T0196125

THIRTEEN WEEKS OF HELL

This Is What It Takes to Become a US Marine

DAVE STIVASON

authorHOUSE®

AuthorHouse™
1663 Liberty Drive
Bloomington, IN 47403
www.authorhouse.com
Phone: 1 (800) 839-8640

Published by AuthorHouse   02/18/2017

ISBN: 978-1-5246-7216-4 (sc)
ISBN: 978-1-5246-7214-0 (hc)
ISBN: 978-1-5246-7215-7 (e)

Library of Congress Control Number: 2017902616

Print information available on the last page.

This book is printed on acid-free paper.

CONTENTS

You are about to embark on thirteen weeks of hell, which is what it takes to become a US Marine. This is a true-life story about the Marine Corps boot camp. It was inspired by the citizens of the United States of America.

PREFACE
BECOMING A US MARINE

———◦◈◦———

THIS IS THE true-life, heartwarming story of an eighteen-year-old's experiences in the Marine Corps boot camp. This story will touch hearts and prompt smiles and tears as well as pride in the world's finest and most disciplined of all military branches—the United States Marine Corps.

Watch the maturity of a young kid and see how the Marines mold him into a man. See the heartache, loss of love, and loneliness that he experienced as he sacrificed for the love of his country and fellow man. Understand what Marines go through to keep your family safe at night.

This book takes you right into boot camp, as if you were there. You will feel the pain that it takes to become a warrior. Your heart will pound as if the Drill Instructors were in your living room. This real life story brings boot-camp reality right into your home.

After you read this remarkable story, you will not have any more questions. *Thirteen Weeks of Hell* will answer them all.

A NOTE TO THE READER

BEFORE YOU START this book, please read the Marine Corps lingo on the following page. Marines sometimes use their own language, so you will find this list beneficial. There is also a special thank you that I do not want you to miss.

As a bonus, I have also included a very special poem at the end of the book. I wrote it, and it means a lot to me. Take your time when you read it. I am sure it will touch you the way it touched me as I wrote it. It brought me to tears, as much of this story did.

MARINE CORPS LINGO

1. **Aboard:** on base
2. **Alice pack:** individual field pack
3. **All hands:** every Marine
4. **As you were:** resume what you were doing
5. **Aye-aye, sir:** acknowledgement of an order
6. **BDR:** basic daily routine
7. **Billet:** assignment or job
8. **Blouse:** jacket of uniform
9. **Blues:** short for Dress Blues; formal uniform
10. **Boondocks** - Swamps, and or small towns
11. **Boot recruit:** someone who hasn't been in the Corps or on the job for a long time
12. **Brig:** military detention center (jail)
13. **Bulkhead:** wall
14. **Cammies:** short for camouflage; everyday duty uniform
15. **Carry on!** A command given after a superior has said what he had to say. It allows you to return to whatever you were doing before he arrived with his directives and or questions.

16. **Chit:** small piece of paper used as recruit money
17. **Chow:** good Marine food
18. **Chow down:** This order means eat, and eat fast—fifteen seconds tops. You do not pick up a spork (combination spoon/fork) until that order is given.
19. **Colors:** the raising and lowering of the American Flag, as a bugle plays
20. **Corpsman:** Navy medic who serves with the Marines. These men save lives every day. I believe I can speak for all Marines when I say thank you to the corpsmen who have helped us all.
21. **D.I.:** Drill Instructor (also known as a pain or nightmare)
22. **Ditty bag:** bag for carrying small items that you may need to save your own life or that of another Marine
23. **Double time:** marching cadence of 180 36-inch steps per minute; in other words—running!
24. **Field day:** extremely detailed cleaning
25. **Gear:** all of your equipment
26. **Ink stick:** a pen
27. **Moonbeam:** flashlight
28. **P.O.A:** position of attention
29. **Sea bag:** waterproof bag large enough to carry everything you own; has straps similar to a backpack

CHAPTER 1

IT WAS THE summer of 1991, and a couple of friends and I were having fun. One set of parents were on vacation—they always left for about a week or so during that time of year—and we did what teenagers do. We ended up having a very small party. We started with some beer and went on from there. The drinking got heavy, and the more we drank, the more we talked about how tough the US military was and the toughest of all were the US Marines!

The way they trained was second to none, and with the overall discipline they showed in their day to day activities, I started thinking, *Wow, what it would be like to be a Marine?* I was a 240-pound, eighteen-year-old who was always trying to keep in shape, mostly by lifting weights, and I was always concerned about the way I looked. What better way to get in shape, do something for my country, and make my family proud. Being able to kick some serious ass was also a plus.

I decided that very next morning to go to the US Marine Corps (USMC) recruiting office and sign up to be a Marine. My best friend had also decided to enlist, and we planned to go on the buddy system. Of course, we were all drunk at the time, and you know how guys get after a few beers and a number of shots. I would love to tell you how the rest of the night went; unfortunately I do not recall much. However, I do remember getting extremely hungry late that night and ruining my best friend's mom's wok. The reason I remember that part is because she was so mad!

CHAPTER 2

ON SATURDAY MORNING, I called the recruiting office and listened to one of the most frightening answering machine messages I have ever heard in my life. It went something like this:

> "You have just reached the United States Marine Corps! If
> you think you have what it takes to be the world's absolute
> finest, leave a message! And if you don't, we'll find you!"

I was in absolute shock when I heard that message. I thought, *Wow, these guys are for real!* It even gave me a little more motivation to go down there and see what it would to take to become such a warrior.

I showed up at the recruiting center just like I'd had planned the night before. Unfortunately my friend had a change of heart, although he eventually became a great Marine at a later date. I walked into the office by myself, scared to death, and without any idea of what to expect. I was greeted by a Marine who went by the name Sergeant. He was a poster Marine, that is, the Marine Corps would use him for advertising because he looked like the perfect Marine, the person you would picture when you heard the words "world's finest."

I introduced myself as Dave, always referring to him as sir. I sat down, and he asked why I was there. I replied, "I want to be a Marine, sir." He asked why. I explained to him that I thought my life was going nowhere, that I needed discipline and self-motivation. He explained that being a Marine was more than that, although that was very important; it was also about a band of brothers who would die for each other and to protect our beautiful country. That was a deal sealer. I thought to myself, *Where do I sign?*

Sergeant was a little concerned about my weight, but he was sure he could get me in, because I had quite a bit of muscle and was very strong, I wasn't in great shape, but I was not completely out of shape either. I would have to go in on a weight waiver, though, and also pass a number of tests before I actually went to boot camp. Sergeant sent me to downtown Detroit, where the Marines were doing the initial testing for recruit candidates. I weighed a whopping 241 pounds! I didn't look that heavy, because I had quite a bit of muscle to go along with my belly. We all had to get in line and do at least three pull-ups to pass one test. I thought, *No problem, piece of cake.* There were about five people in front of me, and only one person was able to do the three pull-ups. It was my turn to step up to the bar and knock three out, real quick. That was the plan anyway. I jumped up, grabbed the bar, and pulled myself up. The first one was no problem; the second one was a little harder; and the third was really tough, but I managed. After the pull-ups we went to a gym mat, where we did sit-ups; we had to do at least twelve clean. The third and final test involved push-ups; now this was my strong point. Like I said earlier, I lifted a lot of weights, at a minimum three to four times a week. To pass this test, each recruit had to do twenty push-ups; that was a walk in the park, I did twenty-five just to show off, but believe me when I say, that was the last time I would show off. Well, there you go. I obtained the weight waiver, and I was on my way to Marine Corps boot camp.

CHAPTER 3

I WAS PUT on the "delayed entry program." This put me on a waiting list until the Marines had more room to train recruits. I would not leave for boot camp for at least a few months. I immediately started getting into shape. I tried to watch what I ate and I ran, starting around a half mile a day. I was not a long-distance runner at all, and I never have been, although I was fast. I was the fullback on our high school football team and couldn't be touched in the forty-yard dash. I was just terrible at long distance. I figured I had plenty of time to take care of that before I left, so I'd just start out slow.

After about a week, I was already down to 238 pounds and was feeling pretty good about myself. One day, about 4:30 p.m., the phone rang. My mom answered and looked at me with a not-so-pleasant look on her face. She said, "It's the recruiter. He's on the phone."

My heart dropped. I took the phone from my mom and said, "Yes sir."

Sergeant said, "So, are you ready to become a Marine?

I replied, "Yes sir!"

He then told me, "Pack your gear because you're leaving for boot camp in the morning."

I was in a little bit of shock to hear that. I said, "I'm not supposed to leave for like three months."

"Well, think of it this way," he said. "By the time you are supposed to leave, you could already be a Marine. So what is it going to be?"

I accepted and said, "Let's do it."

Sergeant told me to pack light due to the fact that everything I needed—i.e., all of my issued gear—would be waiting for me at boot camp. I hung up the phone, looked at my mom, and told her I was going to boot camp in the morning. The first words out of her mouth were "no, you are not!" She was not happy at all.

My next call was to my girlfriend, who was and always will be the love of my life. I told her I was leaving for boot camp first thing the next day and asked if she would take me to the hotel where I'd be staying with some other recruits. I had to be at the hotel by 6:00 p.m. that night, and lights were out at midnight. After I checked into the hotel, my girlfriend and I took a ride so I could say good-bye to family and friends. It was difficult and shocking to realize that I was actually leaving for Marine Corps boot camp in the morning. Very few have the honor and privilege to do this in their lives. The next time I would see any of these people again, my life would be completely different, and I would be coming home with the title US Marine—the most honorable title a man can earn. I was more excited than words can describe and absolutely petrified about what lay ahead.

CHAPTER 4

WE FLEW OUT of Detroit Metro Airport the next afternoon. A number of recruits were on the same quest that I was on—to earn the title US Marine. The recruits who were flying to boot camp with me would become the men in my platoon. There were not very many of us, and conversation was low. We were all nervous and excited to see what would happen when we finally arrived at our destination, the Marine Corps Recruit Depot (MCRD) in San Diego.

When we arrived at the airport in California, we were greeted by a giant Marine. I do not recall his name, but I could pick him out of any crowd in two seconds. He was mammoth! His job was to gather us all together and do a roll call. He started in alphabetical order and luckily my last name starts with an S, so I knew not to correct him when he mispronounced my name. Some of the recruits in front of me did so, and it was not pretty. When he got to my name, he pronounced it wrong, and I just shouted at the top of my lungs, "Here, sir!" I was thinking, *Hey, this guy isn't that bad.* I did not know that he was just there to greet us. He was not our real Drill Instructor (DI).

After roll call, he walked us over to a bus that was waiting to take us over to MCRD. It was a short ride, and before we knew it, we were there. The bus stopped in front of a huge building, and two of the craziest human beings came onto the buses, ordering us off. There was complete chaos, and nobody knew what the hell was happening or what to do. One reason was that none of us had ever heard anybody yell like that in our lives. *What on earth had I gotten myself into?* After we exited the bus, we were told to stand on these yellow footprints that had our feet posed perfectly for the "position of attention." The next thing they did was march us into the building and line us up against the wall. We had no idea what was about to happen. They instructed us—yelled at us—to bend over with our hands on our knees. They were yelling at a decibel I did not think could be reached by a human being. Just seconds after we bent over, the buzzing sound of clippers was in the air, and we knew. Yep, this was it, we were all going to be bald! They had about ninety of us hairless in less than fifteen minutes. Talk about a fast haircut; a few of the recruits were even bleeding. After the world-record haircut, they took us into a large, open room filled with empty cardboard boxes— there for the purpose of storing our civilian clothes until we had completed the thirteen grueling weeks of training. We stripped down to our skivvies (underwear), then lined up in a single file according to size. We were issued our new sets of clothes, called cammies, our new outfits for the next thirteen weeks.

After about five hours, it was pushing daylight. We still had not slept, although sleep really wasn't on my mind. Of course, when it was time to sleep, I was sure that I would pass right out. The Drill Instructors during our processing time we're not as bad as I had thought they would be. What we did not know, however, was that these still we're not our real DIs. They were just receiving Drill Instructors!

After four days, we were all thinking that this was going to be okay. I mean, all we had done was complete a ton of paperwork. We had received three square meals a day and had not even gone on a run yet. Long-distance running was my biggest fear, because I was just terrible at it. I had incredible speed out of the gate, but long distance just wasn't me.

I began to think that this was a little too easy. Don't get me wrong; the receiving Drill Instructors were mean. I just thought that it could be worse, and boy was I right!

Soon my nightmare would become a reality. On the fifth day, we were called into formation, and the DI told one of the recruits to walk behind him with a can of red spray paint. We did not understand the meaning of the paint, but after the first few recruits who were a little overweight got two stripes painted on their shirt—one stripe above the platoon number, and one under it—we knew that this was a sign of the fat bodies. When we were issued our gray sweatshirts in which we'd do our physical training, our platoon number was stenciled with black spray paint right in the middle on the front and back of the shirt. The two red stripes made the diet privates stand out from the rest. We called them candy stripes. This was so all the cooks know in the chow hall which recruits were on restricted rations. The recruits who were too thin were put on double rations.

After our candy-stripe party, the DIs ordered us to pack all of our gear into our standard-issue sea bags and get ready to move. A sea bag is like a duffel bag, but much stronger. We were not that sure what was going on; perhaps we were moving to different barracks. We got everything packed and headed out on a one-mile hump. We were right; we were moving into our permanent living quarters. When we arrived, they sat us in formation in a pretty large-sized room; the floor was hard black tile. This is what we would call the classroom—an open area in front of the squad bay, which housed all our racks (bunk beds).

Well, our receiving DI introduced us to our Chief DI by calling out, "Chief Drill Instructor, Master Sergeant! Here is your platoon, sir!"

A Marine came out from behind a wall with a steely look on his face. What a sight—a chiseled Marine with a look that could kill a bear! The Chief DI relieved the receiving DI from his duties and thanked him for dropping us off. That was the last time we ever saw that receiving DI, and given what came next, I was sorry to see him go.

CHAPTER 5

THE CHIEF DRILL Instructor explained his duties to us. His duties were not to train us but to make sure that our real training DIs were doing their jobs. Then he introduced us to the real Drill Instructors! These were the elite, the best of the best, the Marines who were going to turn us into the world's most lethal, hand-to-hand, combat-fighting machines in the world. These were men who were going to make us US Marines!

The first DI was our Senior Drill Instructor. He also came out from behind the wall with a rock-hard look. My heart was pounding out of my chest, and culture shock was setting in, I could feel my heartbeat in my hands! I didn't know that was possible. These guys meant business. I had never witnessed such discipline before—the way they walked, the way they stood at the position of attention. It was an incredible sight!

The Chief Drill Instructor turned us over to the Senior Drill Instructor and left the building. The Senior DI then introduced the next Drill Instructor. I thought, *How many of them could there be?* He introduced the first Drill Instructor, the same chiseled Marine; then came a second and a third! These were the Marines who would train us to defend our country.

The Senior DI gave a command to the three Marines standing in front of him: "Gentlemen, here are your recruits. Make our beloved Corps proud. Turn these boys into Marines. They are all yours!"

If you have ever been so scared that you can hear your own heartbeat, then you know what true fear is. It is the fear when you can taste metal in your mouth, as if your life is about to end. That is what Marine Corps boot camp is all about.

CHAPTER 6

AFTER THE SENIOR Drill Instructor turned us over to them, the three Drill Instructors went absolutely crazy! It was like nothing we had ever seen. We were all in complete shock. They flipped beds over, screamed at the top of their lungs, turned over footlockers, and claimed we were not doing what we'd been told. That is when I realized they hadn't told us to do anything! They just went crazy! They ran around the squad bay like three human tornadoes, with more energy and strength than I have ever witnessed in my life.

The squad bay was set up with twenty-five racks on each side; there were two footlockers in front of each bunk for the storage of our personal belongings. Each recruit had a footlocker with his own personal combination lock on it. The footlockers sat in what was called the Drill Instructor Hallway; in no way shape or form were we allowed to enter that hallway, not under any circumstances. If we had to go to the front of the squad bay, we had to go along the wall at the foot of the beds. No one dared attempt to go through the Drill Instructor Hallway; it was forbidden! The DIs finally got us in order, standing at attention in front of our racks with our sea bags in front of us.

The next set of commands and responses went like this:

Drill instructor: "Dump your sea bags on the floor!"
Recruit: "Dump your sea bags on the floor. Aye-aye, sir!"

Recruits did not move until the Drill Instructor said, "Do it! Now move!" As soon as we heard those words, we did whatever the order was as fast as we could! After our sea bags were in complete disarray all over the floor in front of us, the Drill Instructors ordered us to put one thing in our foot locker at a time—the exact same thing, in the exact same way, and in the exact same place. This meant we were all one unit and would do everything exactly alike. The whole message behind this is that we had not yet earned the right to do things on our own. From then on, everything would be done by the numbers, until we had earned the title of Marine.

CHAPTER 7

AFTER GETTING SITUATED, or in other words "squared away," we received our next command:

> Drill instructor: Line up for chow!
> Recruits: "Line up for chow. Aye-aye sir!"

The recruits remained motionless until the Drill Instructor commanded, "Do it! Now move!"

Then we would be on our way, balls to the wall to get into formation outside the barracks. Every time we were told to do something, we had to execute the command as quickly as possible. If the Drill Instructor thought we were too slow, he would make us do it all over again. This could happen anywhere from two to twenty times until we got it right.

The chow hall was about a half mile away, and we soon found out exactly how those candy stripes worked. The march to the chow hall was not bad. We even sang a cadence song along the way; it went a little something like this.

Momma, Momma
Wait and see
What the Marines
Are doing to me.
They put me on a silver jet.
The air was cold,
The ground was wet.
They put us in a barber's chair,
Spun us around,
We had no hair.

When we reached the chow hall, they made us stand so close to one another that your nose touched the back of the head of the recruit standing in front of you. There was no room for error. The Drill Instructors wanted us close, so we were close! As we went through the chow line, the bright red candy stripes painted on our gray sweatshirts informed the servers to give us only a scoop of cottage cheese and a handful of lettuce, with a package of lemon juice for dressing. I thought, *Hey, I know I need to lose some weight, but this is ridiculous.* We were able to drink water and, on very rare occasions, some Kool-Aid. Once the first recruit sat down to eat, we sometimes only had about ten to fifteen seconds to inhale our food. For those of us who were diet privates, that really wasn't a problem.

CHAPTER 8

AFTER LUNCH WE returned to the squad bay to put on our physical training (PT) gear. The Drill Instructor had us stand at the position of attention in front of our racks, still in our cammie trousers and gray sweatshirts. Then he instructed us.

Drill instructor: "Remove your shirt!"
Recruits: "Remove your shirt. Aye-aye, sir!"
Drill instructor: Do it! Now move!"

After the shirts came the boots. The instruction was exactly the same, except it was "left boot, now move," then "right boot, now move." If we were too slow, the DI would yell, "Too slow! Put it back on!" The Drill Instructors were at maximum volume the entire time. Everything we did was at their command. You could not even scratch an itch if you had one; you had to learn to deal with it. That was self-discipline. Nobody did anything different; if anyone did, we would have to stay and do the activity all over again. I don't care if a mosquito was sucking your blood, you could not move. A Drill Instructor's response would be, "Well, they need to eat too."

Yes, it is true. We were not able to do anything on our own, not even undress. The Drill Instructors also told us how and when to dress, for example: "Put on your right tennis shoe!"—also known as a *go faster*—"Do it! Now move!" Then it would be the left shoe. Those would be the orders until we were dressed and ready to move out.

By that point, we were ready to head to our initial strength test (IST). When we arrived, we had to run a mile and a half in fifteen minutes. It was the most grueling run I could have imagined. Some people did not make it. I was one of the last ones to come down the stretch, and I heard one of the Drill Instructors say, "He isn't going to make it." If I did not make this run I would be dropped into a physical conditioning platoon until I was able to complete the test. That would mean remaining in boot camp that much longer, because I would not return to my initial platoon, but would start off fresh with a new platoon. Well, there was no way in hell I was going to get dropped into another platoon. I had tears coming from my eyes and excruciating pain in my legs, but I buried it all when one of my Drill Instructors— DI Strongman—ran up next to me and pushed me through. He kept screaming, "Come on, Stivason! This is you! You're stronger than you think! I will not let you fail this test! You are going to be a Marine! You just don't know it yet! I will not leave you behind! Marines don't leave Marines behind!"

I am not sure why that Drill Instructor decided to support me, but he gave me a rush of adrenaline and incredible strength, I finished the run in a flat-out sprint! The DI timing us couldn't believe that I actually finished as strong as I did and made the time. But that wasn't good enough; they claimed I had too much energy and did not give it my all for the entire run. It was a case of not being able to do anything right.

The screaming never stopped, it was constant. After the exhausting run, we made our way over to the pull-up bars; we only had to do three.

That wasn't bad, but it would soon become a mandatory minimum of twelve! Then came the sit-ups—as many as you could do in two minutes. The goal was eighty. I think I only did about thirty the first time; other recruits did more, and some did less. I wasn't quite in the top half, but I was not in the bottom part of the platoon either.

CHAPTER 9

AFTER OUR IST, it was a slow run in formation back to the barracks, and we ended our run with some motivational push-ups. It seemed like they would never stop. Remember, these Drill Instructors trained thousands of recruits, and this was their job, day in and day out. They were the finest of warriors. It was their job to train us to be exactly like them, and this would all happen in our twelve more weeks of training.

During our push-ups, the Drill Instructors sounded off with a barking command—"Down!"—then we would go down and touch our chests. Then he would command with the same bark, "Up!" That was a complete push-up. There were tears and pain through the entire platoon. You can see in everybody's eyes that we were at our physical limits. The California sun was beating down on us, and the stress we were under was almost too much to bear. Recruits were falling on their faces and dropping all over. We never knew how many push-ups we would have to do. All we knew is that we had to do them until we were ordered to stop. Finally, we were ordered to our feet. The pain and fear showed on the faces of all of the recruits, because we knew that this was just the beginning. The only thing we could think about was how much more of this we could take.

We were then ordered into the squad bay for our PT shower. We had to strip, grab a towel, and hit the shower. And, yes, the shower was by the numbers too. All of the recruits were under the water, standing at the position of attention, waiting for the Drill Instructor's command. That's when he sounded off: "Wash your right arm. Now move!"

I couldn't believe we were actually being ordered which parts of our bodies to wash first. This continued until we washed our entire bodies. After that, we dressed by the numbers. And yes, that went for the remainder of our time in boot camp. Right sock, left sock, and so on. After we were dressed, one of the Drill Instructors decided to make a salad in the middle of the squad bay. This was not like the kind of salad you are thinking of. We were ordered to take off both of our boots, throw them in the middle of the Drill Instructor Hallway, and mix them up real good. Then we returned to the position of attention in front of our racks, and the order was given: "Get your boots! Now move!"

We all started scampering trying to find our own boots. Then we heard the countdown: "Ten, nine, eight, seven …three … one, and you're done!" We ran back to the front of our racks. I had one size 10 and one size 8½, although I am a size 9. All the recruits claimed we had our own boots and told the Drill Instructors that we were good to go! We thought we would just deal with the discomfort for the rest of the day and find our real boots in the middle of the night.

After the salad, we were sent up to the Drill Instructors' classroom, where we always had to sit in perfect formation. Of course, we could not sit until we heard the command "Sit!" … then a pause … then "Now move!" Then we dropped into a cross-legged sitting position, left leg always over your right. We did this at least five times until we did it fast enough for the DIs. The reason we crossed the left leg over the right was to get used to the sitting position for firing our weapons. I did not realize it yet, but everything they made us do was part of our training.

No matter how insignificant or silly it may have seemed, sooner or later it would pay off.

We were now positioned in the classroom, sitting at attention, our left hands on our left knees, and our right hands on our right knees. During the receiving process we had been issued a recruit book of knowledge, which was never to leave the cargo pocket on our trousers, unless, of course, we were instructed to have it out. This was our Bible for boot camp. It contained everything we had to know, from first aid to hand-to-hand combat (in which case the enemy would need the first aid).

One Drill Instructor stood at the podium and began to speak. Yes, I said speak. It was not a voice we had ever heard. It was hard and straight to the point. We did not know if he was trying to make his voice sound deep or if it was just damaged from all that yelling. He turned out to be the Drill Instructor I feared the most. I call him Drill Instructor Sergeant Heartbeat due to the fact that my heart would skip beats every time he entered the room. I feared everything about this Marine, from his voice right down to his evil glare. He was not a very big Marine, but he was by far the most intimidating. He and I definitely had problems during our time together. By the end of my thirteen weeks, he and I were nose to nose; by then I feared nothing.

The first few things DI Sergeant Heartbeat let us know about was the training they had in store for us during the next twelve weeks. We were in first phase, which would last four weeks. By the end of this phase, we would all be close, have really gotten to know each other, and understand why we would die for our brothers fighting next to us. That is what we would become—a band of brothers, who never left anyone behind. We would start together and finish together. No mission would go unaccomplished. We would carry out all missions, no matter what it took or the severe nature of the situation. Marines do not fail. The mission would be accomplished!

When DI Sergeant Heartbeat spoke, he was hard and motivating at the same time. I eventually grew to have the utmost respect for him, but not before I got to know him. At first, he just scared the hell out of me. Of the three Drill Instructors, he was definitely the one who gave me the most stress. As he continued his words of wisdom, he gave us information about his beloved corps. It was not our corps yet, because we have not earned the title US Marine. That would come in another twelve weeks. I believe this was a little downtime for us, because they did not want us to completely crack on our first day.

I found out the Marine Corps originated on November 10, 1775, and that I had just committed my life to it for the next four years. DI Sergeant Heartbeat filled us with knowledge and did not care where we came from or what we did before we got there. We were now one and the same. He made us realize that when we finally were able to earn the title of US Marine, that the Marines standing to the left and right would be glad to take a bullet for us. He explained that he would gladly fight beside any recruit who made it through his boot camp and earned the title of Marine; you would honor that title together. You would be brothers forever. Once a Marine, always a Marine. When you earn that title, it doesn't go away, you are a part of something special for life, and you earned it. He was the Marine of Marines, through and through. I knew at that moment that if I had to go to war, I wanted Drill Instructor Sergeant Heartbeat fighting beside me.

During our time in the classroom, he also showed us how to spit-shine our boots and explained that a Marine is always sharply dressed. Our boots always shine, and our uniforms are always pressed. Unfortunately we were not able to iron our cammies in boot camp; there was really no sense in it, seeing how we were constantly getting dirty and sweating buckets, although every night we did put that shine on our boots.

CHAPTER 10

LIGHTS OUT. THAT means it is time to hit the rack. Thank God, the first day with our real Drill Instructors was over. It had been long and exhausting. We stood at the position of attention in front of our racks waiting for the command, and then we heard:

Drill instructor: Prepare to mount!
Recruits: Prepare to mount! Aye-aye, sir!
Drill instructor: Mount!

Those words were so great to hear. We flew up into our racks as fast as we could and lay at the position of attention. I had the top rack and soon became a professional at getting in it quickly.

Of course, after we jumped into our racks, we heard: "Too slow! Get back down!" At that point, we'd have to go back and stand in front of our footlockers at the position of attention until the order to "mount!" was given once more. This went on about three times that first night.

When we finally got it right, we heard: "At ease, recruits. Sleep well. I promise tomorrow will only get worse." When the Drill Instructor said those words, he used a voice just slightly higher than a whisper, as if he was trying to place more fear in us. It worked, it always worked.

It was our first night with our real Drill Instructors, and now it was time to think about 0500 (5:00 a.m.), reveille, time to wake up. We had all been issued moonbeams when we arrived. We actually would not need them until second phase, but they came in handy when we were writing letters home after lights out. We had to write letters under our covers so absolutely no light would come out. We were able to make the light of the moonbeam either regular white, green, blue, or red. We always used the blue light and covered it with our hands, so that we could just barely see the page. We definitely did not want to get caught doing this. This was the only time we were able to write letters home during training. Below is the first letter I wrote, to my mom. Note the frantic writing and the scrambled vocabulary; it is clear that I was not completely right in my mind, and what stress can do in particular situations.

Mom
Of course you are the first one
I am writing. Boot Camp is nothing
like I thought much harder, and we
havent got to the physical training.
this letter probably wont be
that long be couse of the time
shortage. I will keep in touch
as often as possible. Boot camp
will change me and I will come
home a man. We are doing
alot of writing now for moral
purposes but come monday the
27 shit will hit the fan cus
that is physicall training. We
dont got to wash are There was
A little delay there with a headcall
(Bathroom) Tell Kristen, Blair, and Aimee
I love Them be writing soon
                    Love you To
                        Paul
                    Semper Fi

CHAPTER 11

---◆---

MONDAY MORNING, I was lying in bed. I could just see a ray of sunshine appear over the horizon. I was wide awake listening to our three Drill Instructors whisper softly to each other. I could not understand what they were saying, but I knew they were there and planning. It was so nerve-racking I thought I was on the verge of a full-blown panic attack. It was getting close to reveille. I did not know exactly how close, because we were never able to see a clock or to know what time it was. We had to learn to tell time using the position of the sun. As I lay in bed, my mind was racing, and I wondered how bad this next physical training session was going to be. How long would it last? Would I make it? Would I die? Those were real questions that went through my mind.

At that point—bam!—the lights went on, and the yelling began:

> "Reveille! Reveille! Reveille! Drop your cocks, and grab your socks! It's time to get strong, ladies!"

The screaming came from all three Drill Instructors at the same time. If I didn't know better, I would have thought we were being attacked by a pack of silverback gorillas.

"We hope you had a real good night's sleep last night, because we are going to break you today! We could not promise you more! There will be no quitters! We're going to push you to a limit that you never thought existed! You are going to ask your God to take you out of this world today! Even if you were going to hell, you low-life scumbags would rather be there! This is how bad you will hurt! There will be pain like you have never felt in your life, I promise, and we will deliver! Marines always do what they say! And I do promise to deliver and inflict every bit of pain on you today that I can and even then a little more! We are going to show you a red zone that your bodies did not know they had!"

I was terrorized. This was even worse than what we'd experienced yesterday, and we'd just gotten out of the racks!

We used the buddy system to make our racks. Your rack mate—the recruit who shared your bunk—would stand on one side of the rack, and you would be on the other, so it was one rack at a time. We fixed the bottom rack first, making it as tight as a drum, then seamlessly moved to the top rack without missing a beat. This was very efficient, and the job got done fast. The DIs ordered us to dress by the numbers, starting with our PT shorts, shirts, and go fasters." We then received our next command:

Drill instructor: "Line up for chow!"
Recruits: "Line up for chow! Aye-aye, sir!"

This was our routine every morning. We made our racks, got dressed, took a head call (went to the bathroom), and bust ass to formation so we could march to the chow hall.

We arrived at the chow hall right on schedule and lined up nose to head. We then did a left face, i.e., we turned our bodies so that our shoulders were touching. We then grabbed trays and side-stepped through the chow line, where the mess duty recruits put food on our trays. We side-stepped the whole time. The red candy stripes were back to haunt us once again. This time it was half a grapefruit, some lettuce, and a glass of orange juice. The Drill Instructors yelled at all of us: "No dairy! The dairy will not digest fast enough, and you will lose your breakfast during PT!"

When we ate, we were only allowed to use our right hands, and our left hands were to be placed on our left knees. This was a major rule that was most definitely not to be broken: do not let them catch you using two hands! After the wonderful ten- to fifteen-second breakfast—and when I say ten to fifteen seconds, that isn't an exaggeration—we lined up in formation outside the chow hall, prepared for the worst.

DI Sergeant Heartbeat sounded off. "Forward!" Then there was a pause, because that is what we were to execute; that was not our command. Then we heard the command. "March!"

We started marching, always with the left foot first. Sergeant Heartbeat would sing a cadence: "Left right, left right, on the lefty right left right, on the left, to right, on the left."

Then came another command that terrified me more than any other command at boot camp: "Forward at a double time!"

We all responded at the top of our lungs, as loud as we could scream: "Forward at a double time! Aye-aye, sir!"

Then the DI said, "Let's get some!" which was our command to run over to the field where we would spend a lot of our time training. We arrived at the field five minutes later, and many of us were severely winded; the cardio just wasn't there yet. That was like a five-minute mile; half the platoon fell back, and when that happened the Drill Instructors were all over us, screaming in our faces, their noses on our cheeks, spit flying—a true living nightmare.

> "Pick it up, recruit! I'm not waiting on you! Your momma ain't nowhere around here to hold your pretty little hand!"

I wanted to tell the Drill Instructor, *Hey, that was a little fast there, buddy. How about taking it easy on us for our first day here, okay?* But, of course, those words never came out of my mouth. We had actually been in boot camp for about one week, and I was down five pounds, but I really wasn't ready for this. I am not sure anyone can prepare himself for this type of training.

There was one thing I learned pretty quickly in boot camp: we were not actually Marines yet; we were just recruits trying to become Marines. After earning the title of Marine, we would be in even more trouble. Here is a little insider information for you: Marines strive to make sure recruits don't get pushed so hard that they have heart attacks or strokes and die; they do have a responsibility to keep you alive. Marines are pushed even harder, because after boot camp comes Marine Corps Combat Training (MCT), which takes place before you're sent to war. That's a whole other story, and makes boot camp look like summer camp, especially on a fitness level. (That's the only secret I'll reveal about the upcoming thirteen weeks of hell.) We were still civilians, so the Drill Instructors did have a responsibility for our safety. Nobody knew this but rumors spread. That didn't mean they weren't going to break us down, because that did happen! I may have even seen the light in the tunnel once or twice, if you know that expression. It just meant they had to keep us alive.

CHAPTER 12

———⬧◆⬧———

AFTER OUR ARRIVAL to the training field, we stood at the position of attention and were ordered to "left face!" We would spread out far enough to be able to do side-straddle hops (jumping jacks). First we would stretch properly so we would not pull any muscles. When the stretching was over, we went straight into our side-straddle hops. This was always a really good warm up for the rest of the physical training we faced throughout the day.

After side-straddle hops came the sit-ups. We'd pair up with another recruit, who would hold our feet down. This exercise was done by the numbers. The DIs made us sit up as many times as our bodies would allow and beyond. This became extremely grueling; it was not your neighborhood gym workout. Insane Drill Instructors would run up and down, screaming in your ear if they thought you were about to quit. Quitting was not an option; you were to go until you suffered complete muscle failure, and even then you were still expected to try. The Drill Instructors seemed to have eyes in the backs of their heads.

We were then ordered to our feet. My abs were knotting up, and I had to bend backward to try and unknot them. At that point, it was a march over to the pull-up bars; already exhausted, we had to pull ourselves up until the Drill Instructor told us to stop. We were lined up in five different lines in front of five different pull-up bars, with Drill Instructors standing in front of all of them. There was *no* chance of trying to milk it. They wanted to watch each one of us individually. I believe I only did three before I lost my grip. Then I had to run to the back of the line and get ready to do it again. This went on until none of us could do a single pull-up. All of the recruits were completely exhausted, and all of them wanted to pack it in. The only thing we had to hold onto was our pride. After we were finished with the pull-ups, we all knew what was coming: the run! After a quick water break, we were back in formation, waiting for the command:

Drill instructor: "Forward at a double time!"
Recruits: "Forward at a double time! Aye-aye, sir!"

To our disappointment, Sergeant Heartbeat called the order, and we were off There were roughly eighty recruits in formation at this time, I cannot recall the exact number, because we soon lost many of the recruits we started with. The run started okay; it was not that fast, and we were calling cadence. But after about ten minutes, the formation started getting longer and stretched out. DI Sergeant Heartbeat was the one calling cadence, because it was his run. The other two Drill Instructors kept running around the platoon, yelling at us to tighten it up!

I call the other two Drill Instructors Sergeant Strongman and Sergeant Boot; you will hear about them later. As the formation started getting worse, the pain on some of us was clear. Some were gasping for air, spitting, there was even puke at this point, and we had just begun!

After about two miles some recruits started falling out, and I was not far behind them. A couple just fell down; others just stepped to the side and began walking. I just kept telling myself, *No pain, no pain*, over and over. I had never been so exhausted or pushed so close to my physical limit. It was the worst feeling I'd ever had in my life. I couldn't

Dave Stivason

hold my head up, swallow, or talk. Not only was I in excruciating pain, my pride was hurt, because I knew in my own mind I could not make this run. I was going to have to fall out. It was a combination of being out of shape and not having any energy, because of the lack of carbohydrates in my boot-camp diet.

The Drill Instructors were screaming at the top of their lungs: "Get back in formation! You will make this run!" We were all wishing that we would die; it didn't seem like such a bad way out. About thirty of us were unable to complete our first platoon run. DI Sergeant Strongman stayed behind with us, gathered us in our own formation, and had us walking. At this point, we thought that we were getting a break because it was our first real PT. After we all caught our breath, any thoughts about getting a break came to an end.

Sergeant Strongman had us in formation—four across and about seven or eight deep. He ordered us to do wind sprints, forty yards long, back and forth. Then came sit-ups, leg lifts, and more wind sprints. And then we all found out what "getting bent" meant. It is when you are ordered to do side-straddle hops, sit-ups, leg lifts, push-ups, and sit-ups all at the command of a Drill Instructor as fast as you can. A command to get bent would sound like this:

> "Side-straddle hops! Now move. Sit-ups! Now move! Leg lifts! Now move! Push-ups! Now move!"

You would be flipping around like a fish out of water. The Drill Instructor would randomly call out different calisthenics until you could not physically move. This could go on for long periods of time, depending on how pissed off you'd made that DI.

After he kicked our asses, because we had not made the run, Strongman let us know that all of the other recruits were already back at the squad bay, had taken their showers, and were sitting in class. He told us that just to make us feel worse. The pain he'd just inflicted on us had to be ten times worse than if we'd just sucked it up and finished the run with the other recruits. We were all in tears, coughing up phlegm;

many were still puking. The Drill Instructor told us that this was our warning; from that point forward, anyone who could not complete one of the runs will get sent to a physical conditioning platoon and would stay there until he was in good enough condition to join another platoon. That was my wake-up call; not only was I embarrassed that I could not finish that run, the last thing I was going to do was write home to my buddies and my mom and tell them I was not graduating on time, because I needed extra training, due to the fact I was so out of shape. That was absolutely not an option. No way, no how!

DI. Strongman took us on a slow run back to the squad bay, where we would have to explain to the other recruits why we gave up on them. When Marines start together, we finish together. This was one of my most humbling and embarrassing moments. When it was my turn, I stood in front of all the other recruits in our platoon and promised them it would not happen again. I felt so much shame, and if I were them, I would not want to go to war with me. I explained that I would have been more prepared if I'd had any idea how tough this boot camp would be. I believe that they all understood and they also knew that anyone who was not able to complete the next run would not have the chance to apologize. This was a big thing—not being able to finish that first run—it kind of separated us a little it seemed, and the only thing that would regain their respect was to step it up and be part of the team. Marines are not quitters, and there was nothing more I wanted than to earn my title as a US Marine. Of course I questioned myself too: *did I really did have what it would take to become the world's finest? Was I even capable of becoming this warrior I'd set out to be?*

I had no idea the human body was capable of doing what I'd already done at boot camp. They say a lot of your energy gets sucked up by your stress, which was a big factor for all of us. People also say that boot camp is a tremendous mind game, that breaks recruits down and builds them back up the way the Marines want us to be. I can see why people think that, and if you do not go to boot camp, you cannot really understand that everything these Drill Instructors said to us and made us do was for our own benefit and for our training. They did not say anything unless it meant something, Everything was for a reason. There was no time for games. We had thirteen weeks to become part of the world's greatest fighting machine. There wasn't any room for error. It was time to do the job!

CHAPTER 13

AFTER OUR CLASSROOM apology, we showered and returned to class with our book of knowledge. Drill Instructor Sergeant Heartbeat held this class because it was on weapons. He was an expert on every weapon the Marine Corps would train us on. First he went over the M-16, our issued weapon while we were there. I thought I knew a little about guns but found out I did not have the slightest idea. As I sat and listened to him speak, it was incredible seeing how much knowledge this Marine had on this particular weapon. Not only that, but the instructions he gave were clear and I understood him completely; when he finished speaking I remembered everything he said.

He did not miss anything; by the time our weapons were issued to us, we would have all of the knowledge we would need to take them apart, assemble them properly, and fire them at the range, keeping in mind the number one thing—safety. Our weapons would become part of us; when in our possession, they would not leave our side. They would be our savior in a time of need. We were to keep them perfectly maintained and in perfect operating condition. We learned to respect our weapons as we respected ourselves.

The day was coming to an end, and everybody was completely exhausted. We were then informed we were going to have a field day. That sounded pretty good to all of us. *Let's do it*, I said to myself, thinking we'd have some free time to chat or write a letter. To our surprise, however, we learned that a field day was a serious clean up of the squad bay. *Okay, let's get started and knock this out.* Some recruits received latrine duty, and others were assigned to clean the squad bay. *Okay, where are the mops?*

I'm now going to explain to you what a Marine Corps boot-camp mop is. Recruit 1 holds his own elbows while recruit 2 wraps a towel around his forearms. Then recruit 1 lies face down while recruit 2 picks up his ankles, as if they are in a wheelbarrow race. Recruit 2 then pushes recruit 1 up and down the deck, swabbing the floor. Then they switch places until the floor is clean.

That was exhausting and, no pun intended, you had to put your elbow into it. After our clean up was complete and we passed inspection, we were all beyond tired. It was time once again to hit the rack. We all got ready by the numbers and prepared to mount.

Drill instructor: "Prepare to mount!"
Recruits: "Prepare to mount! Aye-aye, sir!"

Then DI Sergeant Heartbeat gave the command: "Mount!" We were all in our racks at the position of attention, waiting for the "at ease" command, when Sergeant Heartbeat ordered us to sing our beloved "Marines' Hymn," which we'd learned earlier.

From the halls of Montezuma, to the shores of Tripoli
We fight our country's battles in the air on land and sea
First to fight for right and freedom and to keep our honor clean
We are proud to claim the title of United States Marine

Our flag's unfurled to every breeze from dawn to setting sun
We have fought in every clime and place where we could take a gun
In the snow of far off northern lands and in sunny tropic scenes
You will find us always on the job the United States Marines

Here's health to you and to our Corps, which we are proud to serve
In many a strife we've fought for life and never lost our nerve
If the Army and the Navy ever look on Heaven's scenes
They will find the streets are guarded by United States Marines

At the end of our hymn, Sergeant Heartbeat spoke in a almost evil whisper. He instructed us that when we were in our racks that we would answer "yes sir" by snapping our fingers twice and "no sir" by snapping them once. We were never to sound off while lying in our racks.

The first question he asked was, did we think we worked hard today? We snapped our fingers twice. Then he asked if we missed our mamas? Snap, snap was the answer. He then spoke real low, in that whisper of his, as he walked up and down the Drill Instructor Hallway between the racks—just loud enough so that we could hear clearly.

> "Well, boys, welcome to boot camp. Some of you fell out of our run today, and some of you made it. I promise you all now it will only get worse. Look next to you, because that recruit may not be here in the morning."

That was something DI Heartbeat always said to keep us guessing and on our toes.

> "The training you did today did not even scratch the surface of what is yet to come. I will push you to your breaking point and beyond. All of you will be pushed beyond your limits and half of you will break! I will weed out the weak, because the Marine Corps will not accept weak people. In the next few days we will weed you out. That's what I do, I break recruits, and if you can be broken, I will be the one to do it. Have a nice sleep, ladies, and think about what I said, because this is the only time you will have to think. At ease!"

It was finally over, my nightmare of a day. I could only imagine what the next day had in store for us. It was almost impossible to sleep given everything that was running through my mind. I could hear the airplanes taking off from the airport and flying overhead; all I could think was, *Man, I wish I was on one of those planes*, and then words of my recruiter, the Marine who enlisted me, came to my head. Before I left, he kept reminding me that the quickest way through was straight through, and that it would be over before I knew it.

I couldn't stop thinking about what my buddies were doing at this time and how much fun they were having. I wondered if anybody at home even had a clue of what I was going through. I guess I started feeling a little bit sorry for myself, because I didn't know how else to feel. Did I jump the gun on this Marine thing? Or was this really what I wanted to do? Well it was too late now, and I realized it was now or never. I reminded myself how strong I actually was. I mean, I had benched pressed more than anybody at my high school. I wasn't going to let these guys break me! After all, those Drill Instructors were once in my shoes, and somebody trained them. Now it was my turn to become a Marine!

CHAPTER 14

0500. 5:00 A.M. ZERO DARK THIRTY was here. "Reveille! Reveille! Reveille! Let's go, ladies! Eighty-eight days and a wake-up! We don't have much time!"

Eighty-eight days and a wake up—that was how much time we had left in boot camp. I thought, *Let the countdown begin!*

After chow, we went out to the parade deck (a huge black-top lot), which was where we would practice our Drill. In other words, we learned how to march properly in formation under the command of a DI. In this case, our Drill Instructor was Sergeant Strongman, who had great rhythm. We would compete against the other platoons in boot camp. From what I understood, the Drill Instructors also would be graded on our performance, so if we screwed something up, it would make them look bad too, and we did not want that to happen. We ended up spending hours on this parade deck, learning all the Drill commands. It was more than just marching; we would soon learn how to handle our weapons while marching. First things first, though; we had to learn how to march properly without a weapon before we could take on that task. After about five hours, we knew pretty much what was expected of us.

We went off to the chow hall for a quick lunch, then back to the barracks to change for PT. Every time I heard the words "physical training" I felt like I'd been kicked in the gut by a mule.

We were not sure what this PT session consisted of, but the DIs said it would be brutal, and I'd never known them to lie to us yet. We began with normal stretching and then went to the obstacle course. It looked huge; I'd never seen obstacles like that in my life, and the ropes we had to climb made the ones in high school gym class look very small. DI Strongman demonstrated how we would do the obstacle course by completing it himself first.

He made it look easy, a lot easier than it was. It consisted of going through parallel bars by hanging and walking hand over hand. Then you had to climb up on one log and jump to another about four or five feet away and four feet higher than the one you were already standing on. Of course, half of us slammed into the log, knocking the wind out of ourselves. But you just had to get up and do it again. That happened every time you tried to jump to it. After you finally pulled yourself on that log and stabilized yourself, you walked down a log that was placed at a 45 degree angle and jumped to a bar that was a little higher and a lot wider. It was maybe twenty feet long, but the trick was to grab it, hurl one leg over and then the next, so your whole body was over the bar. This was very tricky to learn and quite a few were not able to get the hang of it for a few days; fortunately, I was actually able to do it without any real hiccups.

Then came what we called the stairway to heaven. It was a huge wooden towering platform that you had to climb—up one side and down the other. This would have cured any fear of heights you had! The last obstacle in the course was the infamous rope climb. I have never once been able to climb a rope. It seemed like every time I tried it in high school, I would get halfway up and have to pee. It's embarrassing for me to admit, but I'm laying it all out here. Well, that didn't change, but one thing it did—the way DI Strongman showed us how to climb that rope. After watching him do it, I was able to climb the rope. I still had to pee, but I got to the top. There were three ropes lined up side by side, and there was a catch. Three recruits would start climbing at the same time, and if you were the first one to the top, you had to wait for the other two to get to the top before you could come down. For a couple of weeks there were still a lot of recruits who could not quite make it to the top. It was bad when you ended up in the same line with a recruit you knew couldn't make it. Sometimes you would hang there for what seemed an eternity or until the Drill Instructor realized you were going to drop and ordered you down. There was a trick Sergeant Strongman taught us: by wrapping your leg around the rope and positioning your feet correctly to grasp the rope, you could almost stay up without using your arms. I came to love the rope, and after about nine weeks I was flying up it without using my feet. I could do hand over hand to the top and back down. The reason I was getting so good was because of the weight I was dropping.

Now that you have heard about our obstacle course, I will tell you why I decided to call this DI Sergeant Strongman. Some of the recruits were talking and were thinking that the DI had a little bit of a belly. The DIs wore different clothes than we did, of course; their PT shirts were red nylon T-shirts while ours were cotton cammie green T-shirts. It always looked like Strongman's belly was sticking out just a little. After we returned to the barracks, Strongman dumped a canteen of water over his head and his nylon shirt stuck to him like a glove. At that point the question of whether he had a belly was answered: his abs were so ripped and so big they actually stuck out at least two inches. His shirt was creased with ab muscles, and we were all in awe. The only time I had ever seen anything like that was on some infomercial selling an ab machine. That is one of the reasons I named him Sergeant Strongman.

After we realized DI Strongman was not an average human, we returned to the barracks, took our showers, and sat down cross-legged on the floor for class. DI Sergeant Boot taught this classroom session. He told us that swim qualification was coming up, and we had to pass to move on to phase 2. I was not real worried about this one. I could swim. I wouldn't win any races, but I wouldn't drown. Or so I thought before he told us that we had to jump off a thirty-foot tower holding our rifles and a sixty-pound Alice pack. Okay, then I was a little concerned about my swimming skills. Again, this wasn't your friend's pool; I seemed to keep forgetting stuff like that. I heard swim test and thought, *Great!* Then reality hit. I should have known better!

The swim qualification would come just before second phase, so there was no time to retake the test if you failed. While you were retaking your test, the rest of your platoon would be on their way to Camp Pendleton. Sergeant Boot also told us that anyone who excelled in swimming would receive extra points, which would look good in our records and during consideration for future positions in the Marine Corps—as would anything in which we excelled.

CHAPTER 15

AFTER DI SERGEANT Boot's class, it was finally time for mail call. This was the best part of the day, unless you didn't get anything. Before I went to boot camp, my recruiter said to tell all my friends not to write that much and definitely not to send care packages (cookies, candy, any type of snack). He informed me that I would definitely regret it. I took his advice. I told everyone to write but not every day. This kept the DI from calling your name more than he needed to. I received a couple of letters, and there was a big box with all of our mail. I could tell everybody was hoping it was not his. The unlucky recruit had to open the box in front of everybody, and there were enough chocolate chip cookies inside to feed the whole platoon. Unfortunately the DIs made him eat every last one of them by himself. I thought he was going to die; we all had to sit in formation until the eating of the chocolate chip cookies was over. The recruit then went to the head and gave the cookies to the porcelain gods.

After the entertainment, we were sent to our racks. It was time to write letters, think about tomorrow, and get our minds straight for what was coming next. In the night silence you could hear sniffles coming from some of the recruits. It happened often, because we read our letters more than once and usually after lights out.

0500. Zero dark thirty. "Reveille! Reveille! Reveille! Let's go, ladies!"

One of the recruits was not moving fast enough; the DI was all over him and made the whole platoon do push-ups because one guy did not have a sense of urgency. His name rhymed with cockroach, so from that day forward, every time the lights came on, he had to run around the squad bay, like a cockroach would do when the lights came on. He had to do this until the DI said, "Die, cockroach, die!" The platoon always had to repeat the DI's order, no matter what it was. So we sounded off: "Die, cockroach, die!" The recruit would flip on his back and say, "Cockroach is dead, sir!" Then we would begin our day. That morning cockroach thing went on for about five days.

We were all lined up in formation, ready to go over to the field for PT. Our hearts were already pounding even though we hadn't started yet. The run over to the field went a little easier, to my surprise. After we arrived, we stretched and then marched over to a huge wooden podium on which at least five recruits could stand. But there was only one Marine on top of it—an instructor we had never seen before—our hand-to-hand combat instructor. It was time to find out why a Marine is so deadly when it comes to hand-to-hand combat.

First he showed us the combat warrior stance; this was the stance we would take every time we were in class or began an offensive or defensive move. The tactics were straight, to the point, and very severe on your opponent. Remember, Marines were not going to war to box or grapple with somebody. If it came down to hand to hand, it would be fast and deadly. Although we trained on the other aspects of martial arts as well, we trained in hand-to-hand combat always. We put in a lot of hours until we memorized the moves so that muscle memory would always kick in. Our Drill Instructors walked around while we executed the moves to make sure we did them properly. They corrected us if we did anything wrong with a personal demonstration, if you know what I mean, and we didn't want that. At the end of our hand-to-hand combat class, we resumed our formation and heard the Drill Instructor command, "Right face!"

The platoon turned right. The DI commanded, "Forward at a double time!" I was thinking, *Are you kidding me?*

We sounded off weakly: "Forward at a double time. Aye-aye, sir."

And we were off. I kept telling myself, *Just watch your breathing, nice and easy, just keep up, don't fall back.* I thought about the day before when some of us fell out. If I didn't make this one, I would have to die while I was running; that was the only way I would fall out, I was not about to go through the pain and embarrassment that I'd gone through the day before. It would be so much easier just to make the run, especially since if I didn't make this one, I would be sent to the physical conditioning platoon.

I soon found out that there are different types of pain. There is the pain that comes with pride and not fearing what will happen to you, and there is the pain of failure and fatigue. The pain associated with pride would not hurt any less, but it would be a good pain because it came with the satisfaction that I'd made the run and finished with my brothers. Once you passed the physical pain mark where it couldn't get any worse, your mind entered a whole new world, almost as though it was not you making the run. About half an hour into it, you were surrounded by the Drill Instructors, everybody was in excruciating pain, and you had already lost some recruits. The pain was shared by everybody. Everybody was hurting and trying to motivate each other to keep going.

The DI was calling cadence and singing the same words: "We started together ... Gonna finish together ..."

Over and over he sang this to keep us motivated and to remind us we were not alone. We were all together on the same quest. Yes, of course, some individuals wouldn't make it; if everybody who joined made it, the Marines would not have the reputation they have earned.

About an hour later, all of us were in real bad shape—coughing, sweating, puking. Some were even crying because it hurt so bad, but that was the test. Those of us still standing in formation at the end of the run were serious about becoming Marines. We instantly had respect for one another, because not everyone could do what we had just done. We pulled together and helped each other through it. Those recruits who did not make it today would go back to pack their gear and were off to the physical conditioning platoon; we would not see them again. They did not even give us a chance to say good-bye; it was just pack your gear and get into formation outside for the reassignment. It was a reality check for many of us. It was sad to see them go, but I thought that if the run had been another fifteen minutes, I might have been on my way to the physical conditioning platoon as well. I could not thank God enough that day for carrying me through like he did. I am also sure other recruits were counting their blessings too.

After our PT shower—basically just a quick rinse of the sweat— we were off to the chow hall. It was quick and painless; at that point I was happy with anything that did not take much effort, because I could barely lift my arms. That night went pretty smoothly; we were instructed to study on our own and make sure our boots were shined by the time lights were out. We were to have a test the next day on the material we'd learned so far. Boot camp was not all about physical conditioning; it was about knowledge and using your brain as well. We became experts in first aid and CPR. We learned about the human body and how it reacts to certain environments. I could see that there was more to being a Marine than I had ever imagined.

After lights out I thought about my girlfriend back home, I was so in love with her, it hurt. If she came to me today, I'd welcome her with open arms. I would have done anything for this girl and her family. Her parents were great; they always treated me like I was part of the family and I was always accepted. Her dad and I had vicious games of ping pong. We would go back and forth, but it always seemed like he held back just a little with our games. Most of the time he caught me at the end. He was a great player and a great man. Those were the thoughts that kept me sane day in and day out during my months in boot camp. I still didn't know I had only scratched the surface.

I was already seeing major changes in my body. I was just about two hundred pounds at this point. My stomach seemed like it was getting loose. I could breathe well. I thought, *Wow, this actually feels pretty good, considering all the pain I am in.* I felt my abs start to form and get hard under a layer of fat—thanks to the countless number of upside-down sit-ups they made us do. Seeing those changes motivated me. Losing weight was something I had always wanted but never had the self-discipline to do on my own.

CHAPTER 16

0500. REVEILLE CAME, AND I was up in a flash. Finally, I'd had a good night sleep. My rack mate and I got making our racks down to a science—fast and flawless—he and I made a good team. Your rack mate was the one you were closest to. You did everything next to each other; the tasks that required teamwork were done with your rack mate. We shared thoughts and opinions about our day-to-day activities and also our personal lives before boot camp.

When we finished making our rack and got dressed by the numbers. I could tell my cammie trousers were loose. This motivated me and made me feel much better. We lined up outside into formation to go to chow, I was hungry and couldn't wait to get there. To my surprise, my grapefruit and spoonful of cottage cheese satisfied my appetite. I felt fine and didn't need anything else. Maybe these Drill Instructors knew what they were doing after all.

After chow, we were on our way to take the test we'd studied for the night before. The classroom was air conditioned, which made it very easy to fall asleep, so the DIs made us keep smacking the backs of our bald heads anytime we thought we were going to fall asleep.

We did not have to ask permission for this; we could smack our heads anytime we felt the need. After the test we marched back to the squad bay to hear the results; all but one recruit received 100 percent! Only one question was missed. In our minds, that was great, but the Drill Instructors thought we'd failed. We did not know which recruit missed that question, but it was blamed on all of us; for that, we would all pay severely.

We were immediately ordered to line up for formation outside. The Drill Instructors went absolutely crazy, screaming at us. We did not know exactly what to expect but assumed that nothing good would happen. This would be our first run in our cammies. Then the order came.

Drill instructor: "Forward at a double time!"
Recruits: "Forward at a double time. Aye-aye, sir!"

And we were off. This run was a little more controlled and a lot slower than the runs we'd been on previously, I think because we were in boots and utility uniforms (or boots and yoots). They always made us run with canteens when we were in our cammies; that's why we called it boots and yoots, which is short for utility gear.

The run lasted maybe an hour; again, everybody was dying. We all helped each other through it, because many of us were ready to drop, as usual. The run ended at the field where we normally did our PT. Then it was time for wind sprints. I was a fast sprinter, even though I had quite a bit of weight behind me, but my legs felt like mush. There was nothing left of them; my muscles had not had time to heal. In addition, my legs had never been put through such difficult workouts before. When the wind sprints started, we were going four at a time for forty yards. I was halfway through my second sprint when I felt a tear in my right quad muscle, that is, my right thigh. I hit the ground like a sack of potatoes off the back of a truck. I felt like I'd just been stabbed in the leg with a dagger. I couldn't even get off the ground.

The DI on the scene screamed in my ear to get my ass up. Believe me, I wanted nothing more; it was just that my quad was completely blown. I stood on my left leg and hopped to the other side of formation where the other recruits were. I was able to hobble back to the barracks with everybody and with the help of my rack mate. At that point, Drill Instructor Sergeant Heartbeat sent me down to the battalion aid station (BAS) to see the doctors. Anytime we were sick or got hurt, that is where we would go. The DI ordered my rack mate to help me down there, and when we arrived, he had about thirty seconds to get back to the barracks. When the doc took me in the examining room, he told me to lie face down on the table. He took my right leg and bent it forward; at that point, my hamstring went into a knot. I thought I was going to die! Who created this type of pain? The front of my leg was wasted; now my hamstring was in a knot tied as tight as a shoelace! The doctor immediately straightened out my leg, or I straightened it—I'm not sure; everything was getting blurry. Okay, the hamstring returned to normal, but my quad was still severely hurt. Now the medical rehabilitation platoon was in my mind. That would be the same as the physical conditioning platoon. I could not let that happen. The doc gave me some cream to put on my leg and a brace so that it wouldn't move during the night. I was still in more pain than you can imagine. He said it probably just knotted up real bad because it was not used to the extreme workout it was getting. *You think? Jackass! Freaking help me. I'm not any better here!* I was thinking, *If this cream doesn't work, this doctor is the first visit I was going to make!* Not some bullshit rehab platoon with a bunch of crybabies who just wanted out. I was in it to finish. That doc better pray real hard for me, because if his lack of attention put me in that rehab platoon I was going to end his ass!

I hobbled back to the barracks where everybody was studying and shining their boots. To my surprise, my rack mate had already shined my boots and was ready to bring me up to speed on the class I missed. He was definitely looking out for me. That was the kind of guy he was. When I got back, I was ordered to the Drill Instructor's office.

The DI sounded off loudly: "Recruit Stivason!"

The rest of the platoon had to sound off: "Recruit Stivason! Aye-aye, sir!"

Then I had to sound off: "Aye-aye, sir! Aye-aye, recruits!"

Then I ran to the DI's doorway, pounded three times and sounded off: "Recruit Stivason reporting as ordered, sir!"

Sergeant Heartbeat wanted to know what the doctor had said and if I could continue. I told him the doc said it was in a knot, gave me cream to put on it overnight, told me stay in the barracks, and return to him in the morning to see if I could continue. At that point, the DI ordered, "As you were."

This was the first time I ever heard him give an order, and he said it in a normal voice. "As you were" meant go back to whatever it was you were doing.

It was time for lights out again, and it had turned out to be a terrible day. I was now not just worried about completing physical training, but my leg was a serious concern. I really was not sure whether I could go on. I did know that when I saw the doctor in the morning I was going to tell him I was good to go, no matter how bad the pain was. I figured if I was going to get sent back, they would have to carry me! My high school football coach used to tell us that he did not want us coming to him hurt, unless we were carrying a piece of our body, and those were the words I was going to live by in boot camp.

The morning went as usual with a lot of screaming and rushing to get everything done so that we could start our day on time. After chow, I was to report to BAS to get my leg checked out. After that, if I was good to go and cleared by the doctor, I was to meet everybody on the parade deck for Drill. I walked into the doctor's office as straight as I could without limping, even though I was still in extreme pain. He asked how I was. Of course I lied. I told him I was fine and it was just a little sore. He was probably right in the first place that it was just knotted up, and I asked him if he would give me the OK to go back to my duties. This was all I needed and I would be out of there. He began to bend my leg and stretch my quad; he could see I was hurting, and he also knew that I was determined to carry on with the rest of my platoon.

He told me to be honest with him, and no matter what I told him about my leg, he would grant me whatever I asked him to do. I fessed up and told him it was killing me, but I could handle the pain and definitely continue with my platoon. I said, "The reason I lied to you, Doc, and said I was good to go is because I did not want to get dropped into the medical rehab platoon." He completely understood. He instructed me to take it as easy as possible and wrapped the leg with an ace bandage and said to wear it during the day and take it off at night. He signed my slip that gave me the OK to return to duty, and I made my way slowly to the parade deck.

I arrived at the parade deck just before noon, and the platoon was in the middle of Drill practice. I stood aside and presented my paperwork from the doc to DI Strongman. He read the paperwork and said they would not be done with this Drill for about another fifteen minutes. Then he ordered me to begin pushing. It was not a scream, but it was loud enough that I hit the deck immediately and started my pushing. Push-ups really didn't bother me that much because I could do a lot of them, and I could lock my arms and stay fixed for quite a while, but everybody does give out sooner or later. I only pushed for about ten minutes, and then I couldn't do anymore. Doing ten minutes of push-ups will tire anybody. By the time I was back in formation, it was time for school. Thank God, I got lucky and hardly had to use my leg, which gave me a little more time to get it right and heal a bit more.

Most of the time when we went across the base to the building where a lot of our classes were held, we had a different instructor. Sometimes it was the same Marine, but most of the time it was someone different. This was the class where we went over everything that we would complete during our training. Much would be reiterated, but it was good for us to hear things more than once. The instructor informed us that first phase would be over with before we knew it, and we would be on a bus to Camp Pendleton to begin second phase. Everything we'd learned and all our physical training were to get us ready for whatever came next. The DIs never gave us too much of an idea of what lay ahead; most of the time it was just sprung on us. Second phase was going to be more grueling and physical than first phase; now we were at a point where we were in pretty good shape and close to being able to keep up with the Drill Instructors. He was basically saying that first phase was just a warm up! By the time we arrived at second phase, we would have the knowledge to fire our weapons straight and true, and most of us would already be experts by the book. We would not actually fire any weapons until second phase. The weapon was very important; it would be our life, and we were to respect everything about it—from the way it would save our lives to the way it would take the lives of the enemy trying to do the same to us. This weapon was our best friend or right arm; you would treat your weapon as if it were your girlfriend. We also learned about explosives, disarming and locating them; the ins and outs of hand grenades—throwing them, and locating buried landmines by hand without getting blown up. We were also fully trained on handheld rocket launchers.

After our class, we went back to the barracks to get chits (little pieces of paper that served as money). This was so we could go shopping at the PX, a little store that had everything we needed for the first and second phases of boot camp. The DIs had us going through the store in a single file line, and they filled our baskets. We purchased whatever they chose. This was so that we would all have the same thing, and we would have exactly what we would need. After all, this was all new to us; we did not have a clue what we would need for second phase.

At this point our cammies were really starting to stink something awful; at the PX, the DI put a bottle of liquid laundry detergent in each basket. This was good but we did not know where the washing machines were, and we wondered how far we had to carry all of our dirty stuff. That answer came real soon when we walked behind the barracks and saw a long, flat concrete slab of something with water spigots hanging over the top.

We then knew that we would wash our clothes by hand, like they did in the olden days. All we had was a scrub brush, soap, and the concrete slab. It just kept getting worse and worse! Then we'd hang our gear out to dry and come back and get it later on in the day. It felt like sandpaper when you put it back on your body. The DIs only gave you a few minutes to clean everything; three or four recruits would share the same spigot, so you could never get all of the soap out of your cammies. When you had them on and started sweating again, you would start to itch like crazy; it was almost unbearable.

As the days went on, our training became more and more intense. We did the obstacle course almost every day, and we were running further and further and losing more recruits. The Drill Instructors really did their jobs to weed out the weak. It seemed after time they got harder on us because we had been there a few weeks. We were in better shape and getting used to the way things should be. The culture shock was over. It was now time to get harder every day, and they pushed us that much further.

Homesickness was starting to set in on a lot of recruits; some of them just couldn't hold their tears in when they read letters from home. It seemed as if the married recruits had a harder time than the rest of us. Although, as the old saying goes, I should have put a ring on it—talking about my girlfriend at home. My rack mate had a wife at home and a baby on the way. I had more respect for him than anybody in the platoon. We were really there for each other when one of us was at the emotional breaking point. If I was having a hard time, he was strong for me, and if he was having a hard time I was strong for him. We just kept reminding each other that this would all be over with before we knew it. We have already survived the initial few weeks, and we were getting in really good shape. This was something we would finish together.

CHAPTER 17

———◁◆▷———

THIS DAY WOULD really tell the tale of who was getting into shape. First thing in the morning, after chow, we packed our Alice packs with all our gear, put on our bulletproof Kevlar helmets, and set out for the pool. When we arrived, they had training weapons for us to use that weighed the same if not a bit more than our real weapons; this was so our weapons wouldn't be put through unnecessary abuse during qualification. Some of the recruits refused to jump off the platform. I really couldn't blame them, because it was very intimidating, and the drop was pretty severe. That was not enough to stop me, though, I figured, Hey, *These DIs are not going to let me die. Worst thing that could happen is I suck in a little water and get dragged out by one of those long hooks.* They had us get into the water with all of our gear just to get used to the weight we would have to carry. It wasn't as bad as I thought. If you'd packed your Alice pack correctly, like the DIs taught you, it would almost float, and it wouldn't feel like there was a sixty-pound brick on your back.

After we got used to our gear and being in the water, we were instructed to put the pack aside and line up in a tight formation in front of the pool. We were then instructed to swim to the other side under water. The whole swim did not have to be under water, though. If we needed air we were taught to splash the top of the water with our hands before we stuck our heads up to simulate an oil fire on top of the water. This would create a small amount of time for you to take a breath before you went back down under the fire. As long as we did this we were good to go. That went forth without any major problems, but then it was time for the platform. After you jumped from the thirty-foot platform into the water, you were to surface and make it to the other side of the pool. We had to do this twice in order to pass.

The jump went fine; making it to the other side was a little tough, but I made it. I was exhausted, but I was there. There wasn't a whole lot of time before I had to go again. Some recruits were not able to make the swim; they were standing off to the side, after they'd been dragged out by the hooks, waiting for further instructions.

I was on the platform for my second jump. I was still tired from the first one, but I was sure I could make it. I made the jump and surfaced fine. My problem came about six feet short of the finish point, where I should have just grabbed the wall. My legs and arms were still moving, and I was staying afloat, but it was like my body was in neutral. I was just feet away from being done and could not move any further. The DI standing at the edge of the pool was screaming at me to complete my swim. *Believe me, I would love to.* I just could not get myself to move a couple feet forward. I just couldn't get there. I stayed a couple feet from the wall, treading water for almost an hour before they said, "Okay he's good to go." I guess they figured since I wouldn't ask for help and refused to let them drag me out with the hook, I would rather drown than give up. I had their respect.

Before we left for second phase, we had to complete a Marine Corps physical fitness test (PFT). This would be our hardest challenge yet. During a PFT, you had to do at least sixty sit-ups in two minutes; eighty sit-ups was a perfect score. Then you had to complete ten pull-ups—twenty pull-ups would be a perfect score—you had plenty of time to do those; there was no time limit—and run three miles in twenty-three minutes and fifty seconds. Eighteen minutes was a perfect score on the three-mile run. If you completed all three exercises perfectly, you received a 300 score and the knowledge that you had accomplished a perfect PFT. A couple recruits pulled it off and did receive scores of 300.

CHAPTER 18

THE DAY WAS here. We were lined up outside the barracks and ready for our first PFT. I was very nervous, so nervous I was almost throwing up. During all of the runs that we'd gone on before, we did not know how much distance we covered; we just knew how long we were running—and we guessed on the time, because none of us had watches. I asked myself, *Have we covered three miles?* Then it hit me: *Hey, dumb-dumb. You've been on hour-long runs. Of course you have ran three miles. Just relax.* Now the only question was could I do it in the time that was allowed? I did know the only way that I wouldn't make it was if I blacked out somewhere along the way, and they had to carry me off the track. I've said it once and I'll say it again: I would rather have died right there on the track than be sent back to some fat-body platoon.

We started with some calisthenics to warm up, and then we were off to the sit-ups. I knocked out eighty on the nose, no more because I wanted to conserve as much energy as I could for the run. After that we went to the pull-up bars. I was able to do twelve; now I was feeling pretty good about myself. I had quadrupled the amount I could do when I first arrived. After that was a quick head call and off to the track. This would not be a formation run, because we were tracking individual time. We would all start out in a group and then spread out. The stronger runners would pull ahead quickly, and those who had more trouble would be left behind to complete the run on their own. There were a number of Drill Instructors running with us because three other platoons were also doing their PFTs. It seemed as if the Drill Instructors had pretty good ideas where their own recruits were, though. They ran with the recruits who were having a hard time and tried to motivate them to go faster. It was an awesome sight to see these Drill Instructors work. They ran from the front to the back, over and over again. During our three-mile run, they probably put in at least ten miles to help recruits. They were truly the elite of all Marines.

I arrived at the halfway point and was struggling. I still had a mile and a half to go and there was no way I was giving up. Some recruits were already walking, and the DIs were going crazy, trying to get them moving. After seeing that and after promising my platoon that I would never give up on them again, no matter how bad I wanted to walk, I kept my feet moving at a double time! I wasn't even close to the top recruits who finished, and I still had about a half mile to go. I started to get dizzy and was ready to throw up; my legs were rubber, and I couldn't see straight. I was not sure if my body would let me finish.

At that point, Drill Instructor Sergeant Heartbeat ran up next to me and splashed a canteen of water in my face and said, "Let's do this, Stivason! You want to be a big, bad-ass Marine! Well, here's your chance!"

I couldn't understand why his attention was always focused on me. It seemed like he'd had it in for me from the beginning. But at that point when I needed pushing the most, he was always there to push me through it. Sergeant Heartbeat then said, "I am not going anywhere! We are finishing this run strong and together! Let's move, Stivason!"

That was all the motivation I needed. Recruits who had already finished were watching and cheering the rest of us on. I crossed the finish line with DI Heartbeat, and the DI calling the times said, "22:45." I'd actually made it! I was completely exhausted and the happiest that I have ever been. It was truly a victorious day.

After the PFT, it was back to the barracks. Some recruits did not finish on time, and we were not sure what would happen to them, but they were still with us. We took a shower as soon as we got back, and we had a formation in the DI's classroom. The DI in charge instructed us how to pack our gear for the ride to second phase in the morning. Everything was to be packed in the same way and in the same order. It took about an hour to get everything ready, and then we had some downtime. We were able to write home, shine our boots, or lift weights in the squad bay. I don't think anybody picked up a weight that night. It was very nice not to have to hear the Drill Instructors go crazy for a change. I guessed that was our reward for completing the PFT. They knew we were physically and mentally exhausted and over the limit.

CHAPTER 19

⬗◆⬖

The Trip to Second Phase

0500. "REVEILLE! REVEILLE! LET'S go, ladies! Today is the day we go to second phase! Take a good look around, because some of you will not be coming back!"

This was just more of their mind games. They were making us mentally as well as physically strong. We made our racks and got dressed by the numbers; then two buses pulled up out front. They would be our transportation to Camp Pendleton. We put our sea bags (everything that we would need in second phase was in them) in the storage compartment under the bus, then loaded on the bus in an orderly fashion. There was absolutely no speaking for the entire two-hour drive, and we had to keep our heads bent down between our legs for the entire drive. We could not even peak out the windows; they made it impossible to do so. That was pretty messed up, because I had been looking forward to a view. No surprise, I was wrong; they were always pulling stuff like that. I should have known better.

This gave me time to do a lot of thinking. I'm not sure if that was good or bad. I really missed home and was homesick. I had not spoken to my mom since the day I arrived, and that was a three-second call to say, "I made it. Bye." That is all they would let you say. My mom and I have always been really good friends, and this was the longest I have ever been away from home. The stress was starting to get to all of us. Some hid it better than others. I think I put on a pretty good front; I seemed okay, but I was really hurting inside. Your mind is always working a mile a minute. The DIs were constantly saying somebody was getting dropped, and I don't care if you were the best in the platoon, they had you thinking you could be next. This was the big mind game we'd all heard about. You could tell yourself a thousand times that it was just a mental-conditioning routine that the DIs put recruits through. But it did not matter; their words sounded so strong, you could not help but believe them.

Drill Instructor Sergeant Heartbeat was yelling up and down the aisle of the bus, explaining what would take place during second phase. We would unpack at our Quonset hut, where we'd have a roof over our head for some of the time we were there. After our gear was situated and our cots were set up, we would be going on a hump—a forced march with all of the gear in our Alice packs (E-tool, extra pair of cammies, socks, skivvies, boots, compass, utility belt with two canteens and six magazines to hold ammunition) and our weapons. That was a lot of gear to weigh you down.

The hump was only about five miles, and we walked as fast as we could. It was almost a slow run some of the time. The platoon kept stretching out, and recruits began to fall out after about three miles, which at this point in time was unacceptable. We were instructed that nobody would be left behind. If somebody couldn't make it, a stronger recruit was to help out by giving him quick fast pushes in the back. A fast, hard push in the back would help the weaker recruit and not take too much energy away from the recruit who was helping him. There were some DIs in the back trying to keep the platoon tight; we could hear them screaming the whole time. I was not sure what was worse—this or a formation run. Humping takes a lot of strength and endurance. It takes a toll on your cardiovascular system but builds incredible muscle.

This was by far the hardest I had worked since we'd been at boot camp. I was doing well, I had already dropped at least thirty pounds, or I would have never made it. First phase physically prepared me for this. It was much harder, but they had you prepared for it. At least most of us were able to take the pain and suck it up by this point, but some just couldn't do it.

During the hump, we saw a huge mountain in the distance. DI Strongman said, "Take a good look, boys. That mountain is called the Grim Reaper!" It was the largest thing I had ever seen. I am from Michigan; there are no mountains there. It was intimidating just to look at. At the top of the mountain, there was a ridge that seemed at least three miles long. It was named Bitch Ridge and would be our quest at the end of second phase. We would have to conquer the Grim Reaper and continue across Bitch Ridge, before continuing our training and going on to third phase.

The main reason Marines do a forced march is because we are first to fight. We are the ones on the front line. If the Army, Navy, or Air Force cannot give us a ride to the fight, we go by foot. That is why it is so important for us to be in elite fighting condition at all times, and humping was just the thing to prepare us to go to battle for this country, our country, the one we love so much! During a hump, we would do a forced march for fifty minutes, then rest for ten. This gave the platoon time to tighten up, change socks (if the ones you were wearing were too wet), and drink some water. Upon completion of our first hump, everybody had made it. It wasn't the prettiest thing, but we were all standing together at the end. I believe we did not go as fast as we would if we were already Marines, or as fast as we would toward the end of second phase. I think that was just a warm up. Soon we would be humping upward of twenty-six miles in a day.

After we arrived back at our quarters, we were to take a shower and change. We were then to go to the armory to clean our weapons. Before we got into formation, I looked at my feet, and they were covered with blisters. I had blisters on the tops and bottoms of my feet; a couple were already bleeding and throbbing with pain. Other recruits had blisters too, but I did not know how bad they were; it wasn't like we were able to compare. These blisters would play a big factor in about a week due to the fact we trained so much and so hard. There was no time for them to heal.

At the armory, we went out back where they had tables where you could inspect, disassemble, and clean your weapon. We ended up spending quite a bit of time cleaning our weapons and getting them ready for the firing range.

CHAPTER 20

ON OUR WAY back to the Quonset hut, or so we thought, we made a turn about halfway back, and we wondered, *Great, what now?* There was a square building far in the distance, and we didn't have any idea what it was. All we knew was that it was odd looking, and what looked like smoke was coming from the building.

We always carried a couple things: our Book of Knowledge, canteens, and gas masks around our legs. Yup, you heard me right—a gas mask. *Oh crap! That's the freaking gas chamber!* And we were marching straight for it! *Son of a bitch! This? Now? Are you serious? Can't Be! I'll Die in that place!* We were scared to death at this point, and it seemed like everybody figured it out at the same time. We weren't really that close to it, yet we were already starting to cough because of the gas. Now that everybody knew where we were going, the Drill Instructor told us what was happening. We were fifty yards from the building and choking, our noses were running, and this was about to get real ugly. Then we were just outside the building, and given all the training we had already accomplished, we all knew how to use our gas masks. As long as they worked we should be fine, right?

We were lined up in single file so that each recruit could reach up and place his hand on the shoulder of the recruit in front of him. We were instructed to "down and clear" our masks. When you down and clear, you have your mask on, you blow out, then cover the filters with your hands and breathe in, sucking the mask to your face so it will stick and create an air-tight seal. *Okay, as long as the masks work, this will be a walk in the park.*

We walked into the gas chamber in a single file line. We were all shoulder to shoulder, standing around the entire space of the building, and the door was sealed behind us. There was a crazy-ass Drill Instructor sitting on a stool in the middle of this gas chamber, just cooking this gas in some sort of steel bucket, like he was having a bonfire. He kept adding more and more bricks until I couldn't see anything. It was a little nerve-racking, but the mask seemed to be doing its job; I could breathe okay. Just when I thought it had to be time to exit, Drill Instructor Heartbeat—he was with us the whole time—gave us the order: "Take off your masks!"

Take off our masks? Are you out of your mind? That's suicide. We all looked at each other like, no effing way is he serious. He then barked out the order one more time: "Take off your masks!" We all knew he was indeed not joking! We all took a good breath and took off our masks. The DI knew we were holding our breath, because nobody was coughing. He wanted us to breathe, so we would get a taste of CS gas and know what exposure can do to somebody and so that if at some point we were faced with the gas in a real life-or-death situation, we would not panic. I thought to myself, *Okay, here it goes.* I let my air out and tried to take a small breath. It was almost impossible. The CS gas burned my eyes, skin, and everything else on my body. It was just overpowering. This stuff would have brought a grizzly bear to its knees. Some recruits just flat out panicked, made a beeline for the door, and just flopped out, crawling to anywhere they could breathe. Those of us who stayed calm and listened to Sergeant Heartbeat's instructions ended up somewhat okay. He instructed us to down and clear our masks, which we did, and we were able to walk out the door. Only then did we show how jacked up we all were—snot hanging to the ground, vomiting, screaming. It was like a bad horror movie. We were blind, couldn't see anything; it was the first time I have been in a group of people in so much disarray and agony. It took a long time to get that gas out of our system, I could still feel it the next day if I took a deep breath. The recruits who panicked and ran out had to do it all over again about fifteen minutes later. They had to stay and do it until they got it right. This is one of those events that stays with you for life, and you truly will never forget it, I remember it like it was yesterday.

CHAPTER 21

⟷◆⟷

The Rifle Range

WE ARRIVED AT the range early the next morning; that was where we would start our live fire. This was exciting. We finally would be able to fire the M-16 A2 service rifles we had been so anxious to use. We had looked forward to this for a month. We would shoot from three positions. One was standing; this would prove to be the most difficult. The second was a sitting position and the final, and everyone's favorite, was a prone position, i.e., lying on the stomach. The sitting position seemed almost natural because of the hundreds of hours we sat on the floor in class. Remember? The Drill Instructors made us sit with our left legs over our right, and we had to sit the same way firing from the sitting position. You see, everything the Drill Instructors made us do really was for a reason. I understood that now.

We'd first fire from the standing position. Half of the recruits fired their weapons at the target, while the other half worked the targets down range. The targets were built on a platform that rose up and down. After every shot that was fired, the recruits in the target pit would pull the target down and use a small piece of white or black tape to cover up the hole that was made. And then the target would be raised, and the recruit would hold up a large round disc attached to a pole and place that disc wherever we hit the target. This was because we were unable to tell where we'd hit the target, because of the distance we were firing from. If we missed the target completely, the recruit manning the target would wave the round disc back and forth so we would know to adjust our sight. We did not want Drill Instructor Sergeant Heartbeat to see the disc waving. He was our rifle range instructor, and it would make him completely crazy if we did not hit the target at an expert level. He would be all over us in a vicious way!

Here is a trick that isn't in any manual, and I absolutely do not recommend that anybody try it. It is extremely dangerous, and you may do permanent damage to your arm. This technique is for expert-level weapon carriers only, and you must know when enough is enough! All weapons, of course, have strap slings, which is what you use to carry your weapon while marching; the strap rests on your shoulder. Take the butt end of the strap on your weapon and make it into a loop. Then slide this loop as high on your arm as possible, and wrap your arm like a snake with the sling, squeezing it as tightly as possible. This will make your arm fall asleep, which in turn will make your weapon extremely accurate, because there won't be any motion in your arm whatsoever. Every Marine knows this trick, even though it is unwritten, dangerous, and most definitely not recommended for anybody who reads this book. It could cause great bodily harm.

We spent most of our time at the range that week, and all of us got really good at firing our M-16s. Of course, we ran every day and did our calisthenics. After the first week was over, we would go on a hump, at least ten miles out, and sleep under the stars for a few nights. We were all excited about this, because we had not had a chance to sleep outside yet.

CHAPTER 22

0500. ZERO DARK THIRTY. "Reveille! Reveille! Reveille! Let's go, ladies! It is time to see what it's like to live off the land!"

I was getting real tired of hearing them call us ladies, but what could we do except deal with it.

When you smelled the air first thing in the morning at Camp Pendleton, you could smell vanilla pudding for miles. It was from the chow hall. The cooks made it from scratch; I am sure that is why the aroma was so strong. It smelled so good, because we diet privates had not had anything sweet since we had arrived at boot camp. Once I started losing so much weight and gaining muscle at the same time, I was constantly hungry. No matter how much lettuce or cottage cheese I ate, my body always craved more food. What I really needed was carbohydrates. Can you imagine how good the pudding smelled to us? In some ways, this felt like a good thing, because the fat I had was melting away, and my whole body was taking on a different form. Sure this pudding smelled great, and I would have loved to have had some. What got me past it was when I felt my stomach and knew it was less than half the size it had been. I was on my way to looking the way I had always wanted to look—like a chiseled Marine.

It was time to take off on our hump to the destination where we would spend the night. The hump was tough. It was the longest one we'd gone on and not even close to the one we'd have to do to get home. After our arrival, we were to clean our weapons and eat chow. We ate MREs (short for Meal Ready to Eat). Now that was great, because each one had enough carbohydrates and calories to give me the energy I needed out in the field. Diet privates could eat everything in an MRE except the cookie. We had to give that to someone who was not on a diet. I gave mine to my rack mate.

It was getting late, but it was not dark yet. We still had about one hour of daylight, and Drill Instructor Sergeant Heartbeat instructed us to get our two canteens, a washcloth, and a bar of soap. He was taking us out for hygiene. We had to go about three hundred yards, because there were other platoons in the area. Not that it mattered, but I guess Sergeant Heartbeat did not want us to interrupt what the other DIs were doing with their platoons.

We stood in formation in the middle of nowhere, and Heartbeat ordered us to strip naked. He instructed us by the numbers how field hygiene would go. We started with our right arms first and so on. You can only imagine how scummy we all were after our hump to get to our destination, with all the dirt and sweat.

He instructed us to wash our backsides (our behinds, yes, our buttocks). "Scrub it real good, boys, and get in there!" Once that was done, he said, "Now wash your face! And don't even think about turning that washcloth over!"

I couldn't believe it! I thought, *This guy has lost his mind. He wants us to wash our faces with a dirty-ass cloth!* When most of us hesitated, he started screaming and going on one of his crazy rants. He ordered us to "right face!" He then marched us buck naked through a completely different platoon that we had never seen before. It was humiliating! About sixty of us walked directly through the middle of this platoon, who were cleaning their weapons. Their DI even let them laugh at us for a while. Now, of course, it is a funny situation to look back on.

A lot of things happened while we were out in the field. I woke up in the morning, and my feet were bleeding and blistered. I could barely walk. The Chief Drill Instructor was with us that day and he insisted that I go to the base hospital. I asked him if I could please continue, and he refused. I did not want to go to the hospital; when you were in boot camp, anytime you face being sent to another platoon, you were scared to death. This was my second injury, and I was seriously concerned. The Chief DI told me I had to go and get checked out. He said that I had what they call trench foot. I was more stressed than I had ever been in boot camp. I knew my feet were in bad shape; they really were a mess. The blisters were so bad, some recruits couldn't even look at them. I was halfway through now, and there was no way I could get sent back. After all, I was in good shape; there wasn't anything that they could put us through that I couldn't accomplish. I was down fifty-five pounds already and felt great except for my feet. I thought one thing goes well, and another will break. It was almost as if my body was a car. I look good inside and outside, my motor ran well, but I had two flat tires.

When I arrived at the hospital, it took awhile to find out where I had to go. I was in the elevator. At that time in boot camp, I was afraid to speak to anybody, and I called everybody sir or ma'am and did not speak unless I was spoken to! When I was in the elevator, a Marine turned and asked, "How many and a wake up, recruit?"

I told him "forty, sir." He sounded real cool. He said, "I am not a sir. I am a Corporal. I was in your shoes three years ago and remember it like it was yesterday. He got off on the same floor I did and kept talking to me. He was trying to bring my stress level down and raise my spirits by giving me some good advice. He sat with me in the waiting room and just kept talking. It was such a relief to hear what this Marine had to say.

Then he then paused and said, "Hang on. I will be right back." When he returned, he handed me a Snickers bar, really secret like. I did not want to accept it, because I was scared of what might happen if anyone found out. I put it in my pocket and thanked him. He told me that on the floor above were about fifty pay phones. I could go upstairs and call home and nobody would find out; the floor was empty. I was thinking, *Why is this Marine being so nice to me?*

And then he said, "Okay, I have to go now." He told me that he had seen the determination in my eyes and knew that in a few short weeks I would be his brother. I couldn't believe that he was looking out for me! He said I only had to do one thing for him. When I became a Marine and had been in the Corps for a while, I had to do the same thing for a recruit that he had done for me. He said a small percentage of Marines have the ability to comfort and guide; a Marine once did the same for him, and he was passing on a rare tradition to me. He then said, "Semper Fi." I never saw that Marine again. He left me with a great feeling and a new motivation for why I was there.

After the doctor looked at my feet, he did not want me to continue. He said I needed at least five days off my feet. I begged him to give me the OK to train. It took a lot of persuading, and he said that he would OK my training, but if I came to see him again, he would put me in bed for five days! He gave me some ointment to put on my feet with bandages and sent me away with my paperwork stating I was good to go for training. After leaving the examination room, I thought about those phones upstairs. I hadn't spoke to my mom since I had arrived, and I was not scheduled to speak to her again until after boot camp. I also had two hours to kill. I knew she was at work, and I could call her office 800 number and just say hi. My heart was pounding. I was scared to death. A phone call like that could get me put in the brig. Then I really wouldn't graduate on time. I might not even become a Marine. I was always sort of a risk taker, though, so the bad boy in me kicked in, and I decided to go up to the phones. I had faith in him that nobody would find out. I was so scared when I saw the phones, but the Marine was right—there was no one around, not a soul. I sat in a chair in front of one of the phones for ten minutes before I had the courage to actually pick up the phone and dial my mom's number. I heard the phone ringing, and she answered. I completely froze when I heard her voice. I could not even speak. Not one word came out when

I tried to talk. She could tell it was me though, because I started to cry. It was the first time I had cried since I was in boot camp. Hearing her voice was too much for me to handle. I just stood on the other end of the phone line while she told me to be strong, and everything was going to be OK. It almost made things worse. I ended up being able to spit out the word "bye" after listening to her encouraging words for a minute or so and I hung up the phone. One word; that was all I could say. At that point I sat down and could not control my tears. I guess everything I had bottled up came out. I sat there, and it took me five minutes to stop crying. I could not go downstairs looking like I just balled my eyes out, because I didn't want anyone to ask me if I was OK. I also had my pride.

After I gathered myself, I went downstairs and into one of the stalls in the bathroom and stuffed the entire Snickers bar in my mouth at once! Yes, it is possible, and after quite a few minutes of chewing, it was finally gone, I wrapped the Snickers wrapper in a bundle of toilet paper and flushed it. Then it was time to go outside and wait for the Hummer to take me back to base camp. When I was in the Hummer on the way back I tried not to speak or even breathe, for that matter, because I did not want them to smell the chocolate on my breath. I knew a recruit would be able to sniff it out in a second. There wasn't a bloodhound on Earth that could smell sweets better than a recruit on a diet.

Then it was back to reality. I arrived back at the base and had to report to the Chief DI. Even though the doctor gave me the go-ahead, I was still nervous about what he would say, because after all, he did have the last word. After he saw the determination on my face, and my refusal to go back and leave my fellow recruits, he allowed me to return to full duty with the rest of my platoon.

The next day was the big hump. We had a little down time, and DI Sergeant Strongman took us for a motivational march. He stopped us all in a very secluded place and gathered us in a group in front of him. He told us to take a seat. It wasn't even an order. He said it like a normal human being. He then talked to us, not like a DI but as a friend. This was a talk about stress. He told the Drill Instructors' duties. He stated that DI Sergeant Heartbeat's role was to induce as much mental stress as a human could take; he was trained for it, and extremely good at it. That was his job—to stress us out as much as he could without getting us committed. He would never show kindness or weakness. We were always to be scared or stressed when we were in his presence. And in my mind, DI Sergeant Heartbeat did his job to a T.

Then he told us about DI Sergeant Boot, who was new at training recruits. We were his first platoon. That is why I named him Boot, because in Marine Corps lingo "boot" means new. It was his job to lie low and try to keep us sane. When he was in charge of the platoon, the stress was not that bad. He definitely had his moment of glory when he bent us all, but he wasn't that bad.

Next it was time for DI Sergeant Strongman to tell us about his responsibilities. He was also supposed to cause us stress, just not as much as Heartbeat, and his main duty was to make us strong. He pushed us so we would get stronger every day. He always showed physical strength and power. His job was to turn us into muscle. He was the perfect man for that job. He told us a personal story. He was out on the town one night having a great time with this beautiful young lady. Things were going great and they ended up back at her place. He really liked this lady and thought that they would see each other again after the night was through. He thought they really had a connection, and things could get serious. He said he went into the back bathroom to clean up a little. It was about 2:00 a.m. Remember, this was the first time he had been out with this lady. That is when he heard someone come in the front door, and it sounded like a man. He walked out into the front room, and the man ran outside. DI Sergeant Strongman stopped right there and said, "Recruits, I never would have gone after this guy if he had stayed in the house and spoke to me like a man. I would have explained to him nicely that I did not know this was his wife. I would have apologized and left quietly." He said that he wasn't sure if this guy was going out to the car to get a gun or some other sort of weapon, but he was not going to take any chances. He said, "I ran out the door after him and commenced to take him strong," which meant he kicked his ass. He told us the moral of the story is do not go home with any women from California if it seems too good to be true!

He then said, "This story stays between all of us, and it is not to get back to the other Drill Instructors." We agreed and things went right back to normal, with him barking orders. However, the story did relieve a lot of our stress, and we could see now that this Marine was really a man—a very extraordinary man but he did have a heart. It did not affect the way he trained us, though. After that it almost seemed like he was harder on us, but that was okay because we had seen the other side of him. He marched us back to our hooches, where we would get ready for the next day. A hooch is a modified tent; your rack mate carried one half of the hooch in his pack, and you carried the other half.

The hump was grueling once again, and my feet were killing me, but we all made it. After lights out and I had been off my feet for a while, I got up to use the head. My feet hurt so badly I had to crawl to go relieve myself. I wasn't able to put one ounce of pressure on my feet. This was just one more thing to worry about, as if I wasn't under enough pressure. I am not sure how I did it, but the next day I made it on my feet, and it was back to the rifle range to get ready for our qualifying test. This turned out to be a great experience during second phase, and at night we also did live fire with what are called tracer rounds—bullets that almost looked like lasers so you could see them going down range. This was every third round. We knew it was every third round because that was the way we loaded our magazines. We knew the difference between a regular round and a tracer round because the tracer round had an orange tip.

After everybody was ready for the rifle range test, we went down to qualify. A few recruits were not 100 percent ready and had to stay afterward for extra instruction and more time on the range. Those recruits ended up qualifying later that day. I wasn't surprised when they all came back and had passed the test. Our Drill Instructors did not know the meaning of fail. DI Sergeant Heartbeat really took the range personally, because he was known to be the best instructor on the range.

All the platoons in second phase were competing against each other at the range, and we did not have the highest score. This made Sergeant Heartbeat crazy! Because we have took second place, we were going to pay dearly, he said. We would learn how to watch TV, Marine Corps style. I thought, *How bad could TV be?* Well this was Marine Corps TV; there was not an actual TV within miles. Instead, we would lie down on our stomachs, put our hands under our chins on the tile floor, and then lift ourselves with our elbows so that the only thing touching the floor were our elbows and toes. This position was painful, and it felt like you were grinding your elbows into dust. Sergeant Heartbeat wanted us to imagine that we were watching *The Flintstones*. We had to close our eyes, pretend, and sing the *Flintstones* jingle: "Flintstones, meet the Flintstones. They're the modern stone age family ..." This went on until the whole platoon was in sync and could get it right. When all the recruits were singing something different, it was tough. Then Sergeant Heartbeat was tired of *The Flintstones* and wanted to change the channel. We had to suspend ourselves with one elbow and simulate changing the station with our other arm extended. We all fell on our faces. It was by far a different type of pain than I had experienced up to that point.

After our TV session, we had to show our weapons how true we were to them, even though we'd let them down at the range. This was called a weapon bend. Sergeant Heartbeat had us hold our weapons in front of us with one arm extended completely straight out. This was okay for about thirty seconds, and then it started to burn. We did not realize how heavy those weapons were. We could not lower our weapons at all, because that showed weakness. I mean it was as if you had to hold your girlfriend up and not drop her or she would think you were not true. I think I speak for all the men out there when I say you would do everything you could to keep your girlfriend off the ground. Well, our weapons were our girls, and Sergeant Heartbeat was the enforcer. That was plenty of motivation for all of us. We would rather have our arms fall off than let Sergeant Heartbeat and our girls down.

The next morning Heartbeat took us out in the boondocks—somewhere in the middle of nowhere. We reached a cradle, a piece of land that was like a great big ditch. It was about a hundred feet high on both sides. We were all wearing our flak jackets (bulletproof vests), and it was about ninety-five degrees outside. We were not sure what was going to happen, and then Sergeant Heartbeat ran down one side of the cradle and up the other. When he reached the top of the other side, he yelled to us to follow. When we were halfway up the side he was on, he took off, going down and back up the other side again. When we arrived at the top, DI Sergeant Strongman was waiting. He made us chug a whole canteen of water and then sent us back down and back up the other side. Sure enough we were halfway up, and there went DI Sergeant Heartbeat again, right back down and up, as if the laws of gravity did not apply to him. Every time we were halfway up the other side, Sergeant Heartbeat went right back down again and up the other side. I can't even tell you how many times we did this. More than half of the recruits were losing their breakfasts and many were just falling down and crawling up the hill. Just when I did not think I could feel any worse pain, Sergeant Heartbeat always proved me wrong and showed me some. The thing that I respected was that he went up and down as many times as we did when he absolutely did not have to. I believe I lost at least fifteen pounds at the cradle that day, because we were out there all afternoon! I was already down to about 180 pounds and feeling great. To give you an idea of how long we were out there, Sergeant Heartbeat called in a water bull. A Marine Corps water bull is a truck that pulls a big, four-hundred-gallon tank behind it with water so we could fill up our canteens.

CHAPTER 23

TIME WAS RUNNING short for second phase; we only had a couple of days left. The nightmare still awaited us. The mountain was not far from where we were staying, maybe a half mile or more, and we could see the Grim Reaper and Bitch Ridge every day. All we had to do was look. I believe the mountain became more intimidating each day when we saw the sun rise and shine upon it.

It was time to separate the men from the boys. We would find out just how much our bodies could endure. DI Sergeant Strongman gave us a motivational speech before we took off and told us to help one another if someone was falling out or slowing down. He wanted us to keep the platoon tight, and drink water whenever necessary. If somebody started falling back, you were to give him quick sharp pushes in the back. As mentioned earlier, the quick sharp pushes were so you could help him without getting tired. It was so much harder to tighten up a formation that was unraveling than one that was somewhat tight the whole time.

Then we set off from the hut. We sang cadence until we reached the mountain. Our mission was to keep it as tight as possible and get to the top. I knew it would be painful, but I never imagined it would hurt that much! When we were halfway up, the formation became really loose, probably one and a half times longer than when we started. It seemed like Sergeants Strongman and Heartbeat got to the top just after my rack mate and I did, because they helped some of the recruits and then went back down to help more. I couldn't believe it. These Drill Instructors had more heart than I had ever seen; they were so determined to make us Marines that they sacrificed themselves and went through extreme pain to make it happen. I had so much respect for them, it was overwhelming. I mean, we had to make it through boot camp. How could we let these Drill Instructors down after all they had done for us?

Yes, they were the toughest and meanest people I had ever seen, but that was to make us the best. After all, this was Marine Corps boot camp not the Boy Scouts! We are the ones who protect our country! We have to be the best! There is no room for second place.

After everybody made it, we set off along the ridge to complete our hump. It was grueling and really tested our limits, by far the toughest thing I had ever accomplished. Completing this hump was the proudest moment any of us recruits had experienced up until that point; everyone was standing tall. Sergeant Heartbeat did not say anything, but for the first time since we were under his command, I think he was proud of us and proud of how we came together as a platoon of brothers during that hump. I think he knew it when he looked in our eyes and saw everybody standing in front of him. He would have been proud to fight beside us in the worst conditions. And we would fight beside him as well. Conquering that mountain together, like we did, bonded us in a way that is indescribable.

CHAPTER 24

———◆———

WE RETURNED TO MCRD, where we would complete our training. Third phase would be tough. We would have to put everything that we had been taught together and be perfect at it all. After our arrival at the base, we were in the squad bay, putting our gear away and washing our clothes on the cement block out back. At some point, someone pissed off Sergeant Heartbeat. I am not sure what happened, but he put us in formation out in front of the squad bay and ran us over to a giant sand pit where he bent us all—from push-ups to leg lifts to side-straddle hops.

Then he ran us in the backdoor of the squad bay, so we had to run through the whole place to get to the shower. This was up and down the Drill Instructor Hallway. He had us turn on the showers and jump in with our cammies on! Then it was balls to the wall and back to the sand pit. We got bent again and returned to the showers. This happened at least ten times in a row. The squad bay was completely destroyed by all of the wet sand; it looked like a swamp. Of course, we would have to clean it up when we were through getting punished.

By the last run back to the squad bay, there was pandemonium. We were running down the sidewalk in a herd, so we all kind of knew that was our last trip out there. My boot lace had come untied, and somebody behind me stepped on it. I hit the deck so fast, I didn't have time to analyze if I was hurt or not, I didn't really care at that point, I just wanted it to be over, but my hands were bleeding, and my cammies were ripped. It didn't matter, I got up as fast as I went down so I wouldn't cause anymore grief to the platoon, but it felt like I'd torn my quad muscle all over again, and I was in excruciating pain. Sergeant Strongman had us all clean the squad bay, of course, and then take a normal shower. Then he had us sit in formation in the classroom.

Sergeant Heartbeat walked in and wanted to know who had busted his ass outside. I thought to myself, *Wow, he wants to know if I am OK.* After all, it had been a pretty serious wipeout. I jumped to the position of attention, although my leg was killing me, and sounded off: "This recruit, sir!"

He looked at me and said, "Well looky here what just fell out of your pocket," and he held up a pack of crackers from the chow hall.

I was in disbelief, I screamed at the top of my lungs, "No sir. Those are not this recruit's crackers, sir!"

I know no one had ever sounded off to him that loudly or in the vicious tone I used. I thought to myself, *The recruit who really did take these crackers better open his mouth!* I would have had my hands around his throat before anyone could stop me. Then Sergeant Heartbeat asked if I was calling him a liar. He screamed as loud as I had. But I was not backing down because that would have meant letting myself down and the rest of my platoon as well. It was a serious crime to take anything from the chow hall, and that is something I never even thought about. I had too much honor, integrity and also everything to lose to pull some bullshit like taking a pack of crackers. I think Sergeant Heartbeat knew they were not mine, but he had to make an example.

He instructed me to go to the back of the class and begin doing push-ups. All I had to do was confess the crackers were mine, and I would be off the hook. Well, that was not happening. I shouted, "I'd rather die!"

He said, "You are going to push until you die!"

And I then shouted back, "So be it!"

I believe it was 20:00 (8:00 p.m.). I really wasn't sure, but that is what the sun was telling me. I began my push-ups as Drill Instructor Sergeant Heartbeat had ordered. Meanwhile, the other Drill Instructors were teaching class.

Sergeant Heartbeat would make little comments while he stood over me, such as, "Are you ready to tell us the truth about the crackers, Stivason?" I would reply, louder than anyone has ever sounded off! "This recruit has already told the truth, sir!"

A puddle of sweat on the floor surrounded me, my hands were slipping all over, but I was not breaking! Heartbeat said, "You are going to push until you die, Stivason, or admit they are yours!" I replied even louder, "That would be better than lying, sir!"

At that point he went verbally crazy on me for a minute and ended by saying, "Keep pushing!" I was at the point where I could not do any more push-ups; all I could do was hold myself in a semi-push-up position. After about three hours, Heartbeat came up to me and said once again, "Tell me those crackers were yours, and you can be done. It is as easy as that."

I replied, as loudly as I could, "No sir. Those crackers did not come from this recruit. I won't say it." That made him act mad, but I didn't care. They weren't mine, and not one thing on Earth could get me to say they were.

Sgt. Heartbeat said, "This is how you repay me? I turned your fat ass into a warrior! I trained you! And now that you are in elite shape, this is how you act? I will break you, Stivason! I don't care how strong you have become!"

I was thinking to myself, *You have no idea, Heartbeat! Bring it!* I was just pissed. I didn't care how long he kept me there. I told him, "With all due respect, sir, you trained me this way. I won't break." Heartbeat called Sergeant Strongman out of the office and told him he needed a break from watching me push, because it was making him tired. Making him tired?

DI Strongman sat down in a chair next to me and said, "What are you doing, Stivason?" I couldn't even think at that point. I was having trouble comprehending anything. There was drool coming from my mouth and snot falling from my nose to the floor, I couldn't hold my hands in one place because of how wet and slippery the tile was.

I replied, "Those were not this recruit's crackers, sir!" At that point, Strongman stood up and went into the office. Five minutes later, Heartbeat came out and said, "One more chance, Stivason! Were they yours?"

I gathered all of my energy and sounded off louder than I ever had: "No sir!"

Sergeant Heartbeat said, "OK, Stivason. You win!" I thought, *Thank God!* I wasn't sure how much longer I could have held that position. He then said, "Hold a solid push-up position for ten seconds, and you can go!" I said to myself, *Cool, no problem.*

He then began his own ten-second count: ten ... nine ... eight ... He was taking his time; those first three seconds were actually about fifteen. When he was almost ready to say seven, I collapsed. Not because I quit but because my arms gave out. I had been doing this for almost 4 hours! I picked myself back up, got into position, and he started the count all over again. Ten ... nine ... eight ... seven ... six ... and I dropped! He was making it impossible for me to complete.

Then Heartbeat gave me a hint. "Stivason, I don't care what you look like or how bad your form is. All I require you to do is keep your two hands and two feet touching the ground for my ten-second count. Think, adapt, and overcome."

So that is what they mean by adapt and overcome the situation in which you find yourself. He started the count again at ten, and I put my two knees on top of my hands, and he finished his count. I looked like I was crippled when it was all over. I went to the front of my rack and sat down. My rack mate had already shined my boots, and he looked at me and said, "Are you OK? I could not stop shaking, I really thought that Sergeant Heartbeat had broken my body. I felt like I was going to have a seizure. Like I said before, just when I thought I had felt the worst pain in my life, Sergeant Heartbeat always showed me otherwise.

I did not sleep most of the night. My body had just been physically destroyed, and this part is very hard for me to explain, but my entire body would jerk about every thirty minutes that night. That was the only time it happened continuously. It did stop, and the next night I was fine.

However to this very day, maybe once a month or so, my entire body will jerk suddenly. I might be lying in my recliner or in bed when it happens; most of the time I am relaxed. It is a violent jerk too, not just a flinch. I'm not sure if it will ever go away, but I definitely know the night it started. When this happens now, it's only once; I'll jerk and it is over. I won't do it again for a month or so. It's as if you are watching a scary movie and you are startled and jump; the only difference is that it is extremely violent and it only lasts a second. It happened once in front of my girlfriend while we we're watching TV, and she looked at me like, what the hell?

I think I earned respect from the DIs. If there was a world record for somebody getting bent, I definitely would have earned it. It was the worst bending any of us saw in the thirteen weeks we were there. What a way to arrive at third phase—by getting the beating of your life the first night back. I thought to myself, *I hope the worst is over, because I think that you can only survive one such bending in a lifetime.*

About a week later, we were all in the classroom listening to Sergeant Heartbeat. Out of nowhere a recruit stood up and at the top of his lungs sounded off, saying, "This recruit does not want to be here anymore, sir!" I think all of our jaws hit the floor, and I don't think anybody could believe what we'd just heard. He must have had a mental break, because that is just something the typical recruit wouldn't dare say or do. I thought, *This guy just signed his own death warrant.*

Sergeant Heartbeat hit the roof, knocked over the podium, and went absolutely insane. This was a whole new level of crazy. He ran across the squad bay and immediately dumped that recruit's foot locker all over the place. He made him pack all of his gear as fast as humanly possible. Then Heartbeat instructed us to sit at the position of attention until he returned; he was going to take this recruit out somewhere for "special treatment." After about forty-five minutes of sitting there in silence, we began to talk softly to one another. We wondered what the hell was going on, and where he could have possibly taken that recruit.

After almost two hours, Sergeant Heartbeat and the recruit walked through the door. The recruit looked like he'd jumped in a swamp, then was tied to the back of a horse and dragged five miles. Heartbeat told the platoon, "This special recruit has something he would like to say to you all."

The recruit stood at the podium, crying his eyes out; he could barely speak. These are some of the words he was able to say to us: "Fellow recruits, there is no better place than where we are at right now, and you do not want to go where I just came from." He could hardly talk because he was crying so hard. He said that there was no other place on Earth he would rather be than right here with us. He then asked us if we would allow him back into our platoon even though he'd quit on us; he was sorry about that and now knew the meaning of brotherhood. Of course, we all accepted him back.

After that, some of the recruits thought that maybe his bending, or whatever he went through while he was gone, had been worse than mine. I tended to agree, but it wasn't as long as mine, not by a long shot. He was in pretty bad shape, though, so it very well could have been just as bad or worse. It's hard for me to imagine how much worse, but anything is possible.

We never found out what happened while they were out there or even where they went. The recruit absolutely refused to talk about it.

CHAPTER 25

━━━◄►◆◄►━━━

THE NEXT MORNING, it was time for our final PFT. This would be tough, because we all wanted a good score. Everybody left in our platoon could now pass with no problems. I believe I knocked out 140 sit-ups in my two minutes and did thirty pull-ups. I could have done more, but I wanted to save my energy for the run. I was determined to get a great time and put everything I had into it. I ended up finishing the three miles with a 19:10. It wasn't perfect, but it was good. I was happy with that, because I was not a long-distance runner when I arrived, and I had improved tenfold. At the beginning of boot camp, I could barely make the mile and a half!

A couple of days later, we got ready to go to the PX. We were instructed to get our chits out of our foot lockers. That is when we found out that one of the recruits did not have his chits; they had been stolen by another recruit. We were put on lockdown—standing in front of our racks at the position of attention. The three Drill Instructors gave the recruit who took the chits plenty of time to fess up. They even put a box in front of the office and sent us to it one at a time; all they wanted was for those chits to show up. That was an amnesty period. If the chits showed up in the box, there would not be any punishment. After all the recruits went through the line, the chits were still not there.

Now the DIs were furious! We returned to the position of attention in front of our racks, and they started going through one foot locker at a time. This went on for about an hour, and they were approaching that "special recruit"—the one who had not wanted to be in boot camp anymore. Before the Drill Instructor opened his locker, the recruit asked permission to speak to Sergeant Heartbeat, who took him outside for a minute. When they came back inside, the recruit opened his foot locker and handed the DI the stolen chits! You could have heard a pin drop! It was scary because we all thought we were going to die. When one recruit did something wrong, 99 percent of the time we all had to pay for that recruits mistake. After he handed the chits to Sergeant Heartbeat and they were returned to the proper recruit, all hell broke loose on the special recruit. All three DIs were all over him, screaming and barking orders! They dumped his foot locker and kicked his belongings everywhere. Then they made him pack right there on the spot and escorted him out. We never saw or heard from that recruit again.

When the drama was all over, I could tell the Drill Instructors were extremely disappointed. They explained to us that brothers do not steal from one another, and they wondered if they had failed us in our training. They also explained that if the chits had shown up in the amnesty box, they never would have been spoken of again. They were not going to punish us, because they knew the last thing on our minds was that there was a thief among us in the platoon. It was kind of sad, though, because we all had grown so close. Besides, he did not have to steal those chits; they are worthless, and we could not buy any more than what the DI put in our baskets anyway. It was a senseless act that cost him his career in the Marine Corps. Another thought I had was that maybe he really wasn't a thief and just wanted out of the Corps. It's a mystery; he is the only one who knows why he did it. But someone like that doesn't deserve to earn the distinct title of US Marine.

After we bought the things we needed for graduation, it was off to the training grounds, where we would box. I'd boxed a little before I went to boot camp, and my grandfather was the Golden Gloves champion of the South Seas. I was excited. I was going to show the DIs that I could put a serious ass-kicking on one of these other recruits. I had lost just about seventy-five pounds and was extremely fast. I had been extremely heavy before; can you imagine seventy-five pounds lighter and twelve times stronger? We went through the rules when we arrived and geared up. The DIs explained that we would all help each other in a hand-to-hand combat situation. In this ring we didn't know each other, but the second we stepped out of the ring we were not to forget we were on the same team, no matter the outcome.

I stepped into the ring with this other recruit and the command was "fight!" The round lasted ten or fifteen seconds, and I laid the recruit out. He was flat on his back. I was instructed to step out of the ring, and they did not let me box anyone else for the remainder of our time there. I sat out of four more boxing matches and had to do push-ups while they all boxed. That was a pretty huge ego boost, I will admit. The recruit I knocked out made the mistake of slapping my left jab with his left hand, leaving me a two-lane highway wide open to drop him with my right. It really wasn't a fight; he just didn't learn anything while we were there. Or he was cocky, and all that did was get him put him to sleep. After eleven weeks in Marine Corps boot camp, you cannot underestimate anybody! Just about everybody has become pretty dangerous.

After boxing was over, we made our way over to the Bridges Over Troubled Water, where we used pugil sticks, which are about six feet long with big pads on the ends. Each recruit would put on a football helmet and stand on each side of the bridge until given the order to meet in the middle. The object was to knock the other recruit off the bridge into the muddy water. When the loser fell in the muddy lake under us, the winner would go to one side and the loser would go to another. After everybody had battled, all the winners would face off to see who the pugil stick champion was. Unfortunately, I was not as good at the pugil sticks as I was at boxing. I made it through the first round, and then some recruit knocked my block off and I was in the water. This was a good day of training. It was different because there wasn't any holding back, and it was a great reality workout. Everybody had fun.

CHAPTER 26

THE NEXT DAY we were fitted for our Dress Blues. The reason you wait so long for your fitting is that no one looks like he did when he first arrived. I'd lost seventy-five pounds. It was great trying on those Blues; the whole time Sergeant Heartbeat was telling us not to get used to it, because some of us didn't make it. He told us that every day. I'm sure now that it was more of a mind game than anything, just to keep us on our toes. He definitely had everyone believing it would be him. He was very convincing when he wanted to be.

Later that day we were scheduled for a five-mile motivational run. This was a run in which the whole battalion participated, and all of us would graduate together. It was a fun run, because by this time everyone was in superior shape. The Chief Drill Instructor led this run.

The next day we rehearsed for our graduation ceremony, because we were actually graduating in a couple of days, and it had to be perfect. It was very motivating, knowing that we had come this far. A lot of recruits did not make the cut, but we could not feel bad for them, because we did not want them to get hurt or die in battle. The

Marines are first to fight and are a special group of trained, fighting-elite individuals. This is why boot camp is so difficult. They weed out the weak who cannot perform the tasks required of Marines. The only ones left are the ones who are capable of watching each other's backs and protecting this country we all love so much.

I was in incredible shape, and there was nothing I could not do. My confidence had risen to a level beyond words. I had just completed the world's toughest training and firmly believed the worst was over.

We were all in formation lined up for chow, when I noticed a brand new recruit. I saw the fear in his eyes. He was a big recruit and looked like he was in pretty good shape. Then I realized I knew him. One day, back in high school, he planned to kick my ass for no reason. He was a year older than I was and had me scared to death that day! I never forgot that moment, because I did not provoke him in any way whatsoever. He was just a bully, and I despised bullies.

Drill Instructor Sergeant Heartbeat saw my eyes on this recruit and said, "What are you doing, Stivason! Do you think that recruit is cute or something!" He then said in a normal voice, "Why are you eyeballing that recruit?"

I explained that the recruit had been the bully of my high school, and I just wanted to give him a "don't f*** with me" look.

Sergeant Heartbeat said, "I'll do you one better than that, Stivason. Not only have you earned it, at this point you can take him strong!" He went over to the recruit's DI, said something to him, then called me over.

Sergeant Heartbeat said, "Stivason, you have ninety seconds. Bend this recruit, and make him sweat! Do it! Now move!"

I took full advantage of the situation and bent this recruit in front of hundreds of other recruits. I tortured him for the full ninety seconds—mostly push-ups but also side-straddle hops, leg lifts, and sit-ups, I made him look like he'd just gotten out of a pool. It was great! I think I was happier than anything though, because Sergeant Heartbeat had done that for me. It was an awesome feeling to know he'd done me that favor.

It meant a lot to me. I am sure that other recruit didn't feel the same way, but he still had thirteen weeks to think about what he'd done to me back in school. Maybe that taught him a lesson, maybe it didn't, but it definitely showed that what goes around, comes around. I probably wouldn't want to run into him now.

CHAPTER 27

IT WAS THE night before graduation, and it was a special night for all. The families who flew to California to see our ceremony were invited to the Drill Instructors' dinner. There would be wonderful food and drink; our families would also have plenty of time to talk to our Drill Instructors and get to know them pretty well. The DIs also, of course, would speak about the individual experiences they'd had with all of us.

The Drill Instructors left for the event early, after giving us instructions for the morning. DI Sergeant Heartbeat came back at 2100 (9:00 p.m.) to make sure we had lights out and order us into our racks. He took his famous walk up and down the Drill Instructor Hallway and told us that some recruits had not made it. Again this had to be a mind game; we had ten hours left, but the DIs had you so rattled you couldn't help but think, *Could he be talking about me?*

It was very difficult to get to sleep that night. Everything that had gone on since we had been there raced through our heads. It was finally here. We had nine hours before we woke up and put on those Dress Blues! How could anyone sleep with that kind of excitement rushing through their blood? I finally dozed off and then about 0100 (1:00 a.m.)

I felt somebody breathing directly in my face, smelling like he'd just had ten beers. I opened my eyes and almost pissed myself. It was Sergeant Heartbeat two inches from my nose. He said, in a low, evil whisper, "Get your PT gear on, boy. Then get your ass over to the Chief Drill Instructor's door."

I jumped out of the rack and was there in seconds, standing at the position of attention. My mind was racing, and I couldn't figure out for the life of me what was going to happen. He stood directly in front of me, put his face right up to mine, and said, "Your mom and your two sisters are standing on the other side of that door right now. They are two feet away from you. I told them that I would bring them to see you if they wanted, and they said yes."

He then said, "Now, I am going to tell you something, Stivason." He was still whispering because he did not want to wake up any other recruits. "I will allow you to see them if you want. But remember you are still a civilian, and you will not be a Marine until you graduate in the morning. You still have not earned the title of Marine. You are still not a Marine, so now that being said, do you want to see them now, before you are a Marine? They are only two feet away. Or do you want to see them tomorrow with the title Marine and when you are in your Dress Blues?"

I thought real hard for a second and said, "This recruit will wait until tomorrow, sir, when he is a Marine."

He said, "Good! Get your ass back in the rack!"

I was lying there, thinking, *Man, this guy just won't quit messing with me.* After all, I was the one who improved the most. Why had he given me the hardest time? Now it was next to impossible to sleep. I mean my mom and my two sisters were standing right on the other side of the door, and I didn't open it. I wanted to open the door so bad, but seeing them after I had earned the title Marine would be so much better. The first time they saw me, I wanted to be in my Dress Blues and looking like the Marine I'd set out to be, not in PT gear.

About a half hour later, I was lying in my rack wide awake, and Sergeant Boot came in the door. He walked over to my rack and talked to me like a friend. He told me that Sergeant Heartbeat was most impressed with me and the changes I had made; that was one of the reasons he had been so hard on me during boot camp. He said that Heartbeat paid special attention to me because he saw me as one of the most motivated recruits he had ever trained, and had seen more heart in me than he ever had in anyone else. Sergeant Boot said, "Everything he did to you during your training was for your own benefit. He wanted to make you stronger than any recruit he has ever trained."

Now that made me feel great! He actually didn't hate me after all. He was just making me a Marine!

Sergeant Boot told me to get some sleep, because we had a big day in front of us tomorrow.

CHAPTER 28

0500. 5:00 A.M. "REVEILLE! REVEILLE! LET'S go, recruits! Today is the day!"

One more time I heard DI Sergeant Heartbeat scream those famous words. They were a little different this time. It was Private Stivason instead of recruit. This was the first time anybody in the platoon was actually called a private and not a recruit.

DI Heartbeat sounded off: "Private Stivason!"

The whole platoon sounded off too, after hesitating for just a second, because this was the first time we'd heard anyone called by rank: "Private Stivason! Aye-aye, sir!"

Then it was my turn: "Private Stivason! Aye-aye, sir! Aye-aye, recruits!" I ran to the Drill Instructor's office and pounded three times, sounding off: "Private Stivason reporting as ordered, sir!"

DI Heartbeat said, "Get in here!" I walked into the office and stood at the position of attention. I had no idea what this was about but thought it had something to do with what had happened the night before. Sergeant Strongman told me to stand at ease. Then Sergeant

Heartbeat ordered me back to the position of attention immediately. He walked back and forth in front of me, without saying anything.

Then he said, "Your sister likes to drink a lot, doesn't she, Stivason?" I replied with normal sounding "yes sir."

He said, "Do you know the reason I look like shit, Stivason?" I said, "I have a pretty good idea, sir."

He said, "Your sister did this to me," and the reason he looked like shit was her fault! He'd gotten a pretty bad hangover from partying with my sister. At that point, I had a little smirk on my face because I thought it was pretty humorous.

Then Sergeant Heartbeat said, "Your sister is a real attractive young lady and I want to take her out." My mom, my two sisters, and I were staying in California for the weekend before I went home for ten days of leave, and he knew that she was available. Heartbeat said, "I will take her out, we will go to downtown Hollywood, and I will show her a real good time and take good care of her."

I didn't like the tone of his voice. He sounded like a guy who wanted to take advantage of my sister. I got angry. I said, "With all due respect, sir, this private's sister can take care of herself, in case you didn't notice!" *Oh shit, did I really just say that?*

At that instant, he went crazy! He jumped up and down and ran around the office, screaming, "Oh, Stivason is a big, bad Marine today! He thinks he can take me strong!" Sergeant Heartbeat started putting on his shoes because, he said, we were going to settle this outside like a couple of real Marines.

He opened the door to his office and sounded off to the other recruits: "Private Stivason thinks he can take me strong! What do you think, recruits?"

Of course, they all sounded off with a big "no sir!" Sergeant Heartbeat then said, "We are going outside, Stivason. We are going to find out how bad you have really become!"

I thought to myself, *Damn, I was so close. All I had to do was keep my mouth shut, and I was home free. Well, here we go.* I followed him quickly to the back door. I wasn't sure what to expect when we got outside, but I was prepared to defend myself. If he was going to kick my ass, he would most likely be victorious, but I promise you he would definitely know he was in a fight!

When the door closed behind us, he changed completely. A big smile came across his face, and he spoke to me like a normal human being, shook my hand like a man, and said, "Stivason, you passed!"

Passed? Passed what? I thought, *This guy was nuts!* He said he wanted to put on one last good show for the recruits, and I was his Marine. He said, "I really did have a great time with your family last night and I think they are great people. I know that they have never been to California before and I just wanted to show your sister around Hollywood." I took a second to breathe and told him I would see what I could do. He then shook my hand once more and said that I was a great recruit and that he was proud to call me a Marine!

We put on our Dress Blues and marched over to the parade deck. The overwhelming feeling of accomplishment was almost too much to handle. It was a proud day for everybody. When we marched out onto that parade deck and saw all of the families, it was incredible. Electricity was in the air. The Marine who announced the ceremony said at one point how physically fit we all were and that we were twelve times stronger now than what we were when we arrived. It was beautiful.

As we marched in formation, we were given the order "eyes right!" That is when we looked at all the families in the stands. We could only scan with our eyes, though, because of the perfection of our marching. Every head was facing the same direction. Of course I was looking for my family, and that is when my little sister spotted me. She had a huge smile and pointed me out to my mom and other sister. I had to take my eyes off of them, because I started to tear up, and that was not happening on that day!

After some long speeches and many motivational words, they pronounced us all a band of brothers and said, "Congratulations, Marines! You are dismissed!"

A SPECIAL THANKS

I WOULD LIKE to send a special thank you to all the Marines with whom I served. It was an honor and a privilege to serve our country together. There are too many names to list but you know who you are.

I also thank all of our armed forces overseas for doing their job—not just the Marines but all the branches of the military. I get tears in my eyes and choked up when I see everything you do over there for our country. You truly are heroes! I did my job and still wish there was some way I could take some pressure off of you all. The whole country is overwhelmed with pride because of you!

Stay safe and Godspeed.

THE POEM

THIS POEM CAME to me while I was thinking about what military families go through while they are lying in bed at night.

At night

I can only imagine
How hurt God must be
Watching his children perish
In a brutal war
Beneath his feet.

I can only imagine
All the prayers God has received
For keeping our families safe
And walking with the ones who believe.

I can only imagine
What God has in store;
It will not go in vain
For his prayers are not ignored.

I can only imagine
All of the families who have lost,
All of the prayers, wishing, and hoping—
Did they have to come at such a cost?

I can only imagine
At the point that we will send,
And where we will all be
When this war comes to an end.

AUTHOR BIOGRAPHY

DAVID STIVASON WAS born in Grosse Pointe, Michigan, and grew up in nearby Sterling Heights. He graduated from Sterling Heights High School, where he played almost every sport, including hockey, football, baseball, and racquetball. He is especially proud of his mother's athletic ability at racquetball; although they have played many games, he has never beaten her. Shortly after high school, Stivason became a US Marine. His remarkable story describes what it takes to become a US Marine combat warrior and will be followed by another book, What It Takes to Stay a Marine.

Printed in the United States
By Bookmasters